How I Changed My Gender
From Female To Male

Thomas Underwood

HOW I CHANGED MY GENDER FROM FEMALE TO MALE:
THE COMPLETE STORY OF MY TRANSITION WITH HELPFUL ADVICE AND TIPS FOR OTHERS ON THE SAME JOURNEY

THOMAS UNDERWOOD

Published by Transitions Publishing
Copyright © Thomas Underwood, 2015
ISBN: 978-0-9940535-2-7

Disclaimer: The author of this book is not a medical professional. None of the content of this book should be construed as medical advice. For medical advice, please consult a medical professional. The author and publisher are not responsible for the actions of any reader who chooses to treat this book as medical advice.

Contents

WELCOME TO THE MOST EXCITING JOURNEY OF YOUR LIFE: YOUR JOURNEY TO YOU

Deciding to transition gender is likely to be the biggest decision you will ever make in your life. It's up there with deciding to get married or have children: it will change your life irrevocably – and based on research, it will most likely change it for the better. Most people who have transitioned gender attest that it made them much happier. I know that for me, it is the best thing I ever did for myself. Nevertheless, it was a very difficult and challenging journey, emotionally and physically.

Because it is such an enormous change and such a long journey, when we go through gender transition we usually need a lot of help and guidance. When I began to become outwardly the man I always was inside, I found myself stymied by a lot of simple, everyday issues. For example, I didn't know how to shave properly, or how to speak to the barber, and I was very nervous about going into the men's washroom. There were dozens of situations in which I did not feel confident as a man. At times I even felt like a gender imposter. Which was odd, as I had been feeling like a gender imposter for so many years living as a woman! Since I've been living as a man, I have observed many fathers teaching their sons how to be men, and it's made me realize how much I missed out on by being raised in the wrong gender. I was not taught how to be a man; I have had to teach myself. It has not been an easy journey.

There are so many things boys learn while growing up that I missed out on. Who is to teach a forty-year-old man how to shave? Certainly not my father, who is long gone. Not my brother, who does not understand who I am. So I have sought advice from friends, real life support groups, online support groups, websites, and books. I have also spent the last fourteen years going through my transition, and I have learned a great deal from this experience.

1

Having lived now as both a woman and a man, I have noticed that there are major differences in the way people treat women and men. Of course, we all know this in a theoretical way, but it has been quite startling to experience it personally. Inside my head I am still very much the same person, so it is really very strange to be treated so differently. I have shared many of those experiences. It's a good idea to prepare yourself for them. It is not just you who is going to change – everyone around you will change too, because they will perceive you differently, and they will act accordingly.

This is especially true of people who will only meet you after your transition. People who originally know you as a woman will be more likely to cling onto that perception of you. It seems to be very difficult for many people to truly accept gender transition on a deep, psychological level. Even now that I look one hundred percent male, some people who knew me before will sometimes refer to me as "she." And some people who knew me before will *always* refer to me as "she" – which is intensely annoying, but I cannot change it.

When transitioning it is usual to need lots of help and advice, so don't be ashamed of needing help. It's a normal and healthy part of your transition. This book will provide some of the guidance that I wish I had had when I started my journey. I will share how I experienced my journey. Beyond that, I have also provided a list of other resources that you can consult.

I am not a medical doctor and I am not a psychologist. This book is written purely from the perspective of a person who has gone through the experience of transitioning from female to male. It has been a successful transition, in that I now live full-time as a man, and I am accepted as male wherever I go. And it has been a successful transition in that I now feel happy and relaxed in my own skin. It's never going to be perfect, because physically I will never be perfect. But I do feel like I have become, for the most part, and as much as I can achieve in this lifetime, the man I was always meant to be. I believe my personal experience will be helpful for people planning to transition from female to male, or in the process of that transition.

There are many differences in the way people talk about the subject matter of this book. I write in the way I think and talk. For example, some people might say that FTMs do not become men, because they always *were* men (internally). I prefer to see my transition as a *process of becoming* (externally) the man I was always meant to be – taking on the external appearance of the invisible man who lived inside my head. This is the way I conceptualize my journey, and so this is the way I write about it. My choices with regard to terminology and conceptualization are not meant to cause offence to those who choose to use different terminology and conceptualization. Neither are they meant to imply that my ways are correct or better than other ways. They are simply the ways that make sense for me.

Some people use the term "gender transition" to mean changing one's outward social gender presentation, and reserve the term "sex reassignment" for people who have surgery to alter their genitals (Kailey). In this book, the term gender transition is meant to cover both of those possibilities. This book is intended for all kinds of transmen, regardless of which kind of medical interventions they use to achieve their goals (and some men manage to achieve transition without any medical interventions at all).

Many people now use the term *gender-confirming surgeries* rather than gender reassignment surgeries. Chicago's Dr. Schechter states:

"I call it gender confirmation surgery because I believe that out of the myriad labels I've heard for the procedure – sex reassignment surgery, gender reassignment surgery, and sex change operation, to name but a few – none is as accurate when it comes to describing what is actually taking place as gender confirmation surgery."

For me, most, if not all, of the other names used for the procedure – or, more accurately, the family of procedures – suggest that a person is making a choice to switch genders. From the hundreds of discussions I've had with individuals over the years, nothing could be further from the truth. This is not about choice; it's about using surgery as one of the therapeutic tools to enable people to be comfortable with their gendered self.

Merriam-Webster's defines 'confirmation' as follows: 'confirming proof; corroboration; the process of supporting a statement by evidence.' That said, if such surgery helps confirm the way a person feels he or she was meant to be, shouldn't the name reflect that truth?"

I agree entirely with Dr. Schechter. That said, I nonetheless tend to use a variety of terms to describe the surgeries we choose. None of them is meant to be anything but respectful of the variety of experiences we go through.

I refer to men who were born with male bodies as bio men, and sometimes as non-transmen, to distinguish them from men like me who were born with female bodies. Some people use the term "cis" men, but I have not used this because many people don't know what it means.

Medical treatment for FTMs used to be referred to as "having a sex change," and is still commonly referred to in that way by the general population. However, the preferred term is now "gender transition", and the person going through this process is referred to as "transitioning."

CHAPTER 1: WHAT IS A FEMALE TO MALE TRANSSEXUAL (FTM)?

Female to male transsexuals (FTMs) are people born in bodies that are biologically female, who believe that we are in fact men, and who may take steps to bring our physical bodies into alignment with that belief about ourselves. For us, our gender identity (how we feel) is male, regardless of how our physical bodies appear to others (how we look). Very often, our gender expression (how we act) has been at odds with our physical bodies from our earliest memories: we were designated as "tomboys," and if we were lucky, we were tolerated.

My earliest memories are of being bullied by other boys because they perceived me as a girl who dared to dress and act "like a boy." As soon as I was old enough to assert myself (around the age of three), I refused to wear the dresses my mother gave me, and instead insisted on wearing my brother's clothes. My hair was always cut short, and I spent my childhood being a boy, as far as I was able. Most of my memories of my childhood are of long, sunny days, riding my bike through the bush with my dog running behind me; fishing for fish and tadpoles in the canals; working out and trying to build muscles like my hero, Bruce Wayne. Bruce Wayne was a little boy who transformed himself into the Batman through sheer strength of will, in response to the outrageous tragedy he suffered when his parents were killed. I was a child trying to transform myself into a man, in response to the outrageous tragedy of my birth: being born as a boy in a girl's body.

Sadly, my quest was nowhere near as successful as Bruce Wayne's. Naturally, given society in the sixties, my parents tried very hard to get me to behave like a "normal girl." I remember vividly the Christmas I begged and pleaded for an electric car set, and was given an enormous walkie-talkie doll. In retrospect I know that I was a privileged child to get any kind of expensive gift for Christmas. My parents weren't wealthy, and that doll was a gift of love that must have cost them dearly. They gave it to me with love, trying to help me to move towards what they saw as my true destiny. But I experienced it as a massive slap in the face.

As a boy, I felt deeply humiliated at being given a huge, ugly, in-your-face doll. I remember going to the neighbor's house. Aaron was a boy the same age as me, and he had been given the electric car set I had wanted. I hung back in the group of excited children, trying not to cry, because big boys don't cry. Then I went home and hid the ugly doll where no one would ever see my shame. I can still see its face, which I experienced as malevolently ugly, although I am sure it was no such thing. The doll's face haunted me for years, a reminder of all that was expected of me – the female destiny that repelled and frightened me. I knew in every fiber of my being that I could not be the girl my parents wanted me to be.

To be fair, my parents let me be a boy for much of my childhood. On one occasion my mother asked the family doctor if she should be worried about my behaviors, and he reassured her that being a "tomboy" was a phase I would grow out of. I have always been thankful for that. That was a time when some transgendered children were being sent to mental institutions for corrective training. This "treatment" sometimes ended in the child committing suicide. Thanks to that doctor, I escaped such treatment.

Although to be fair to my parents, I don't believe they would have gone so far as to institutionalize me. There were four of us children, and by and large we were left to grow up like wild weeds rather than hothouse prized orchids. My father would even buy me Matchbox cars occasionally. Some of my happiest memories of childhood are of returning from the family shopping, crawling around on the back seat of the car with my new toy car. Of course, that was back in the days when no one wore seat belts!

Socially my life was complex pretty much from the time I learned to walk. I played with the boys as much as they would let me, but they tended to reject me whenever possible. On one occasion I remember running up a ramp in an empty parking garage, clutching my wooden go kart under my arm. The other boys were racing down the ramp from the roof to the road on their go karts. I had just finished making my own kart, and I was excited about joining them. They looked up at me suspiciously as I approached. There was a strange primal moment in which they all looked at each other, and then as one, they all bent down to pick up stones (the roof had some kind of gravel finish, so there were lots of little stones lying around). As I got closer they started to throw the stones at me. My brother was with them. He hesitated for a moment, looking from me to the boys and back again, and then he slowly bent to pick up a stone and join them.

So much for the stereotype of the protective brother. In that tense moment, my brother decided to join the normal majority, and reject the child who was transgressing all of the societal norms – even if that child was his sibling. I ran away, scorned and shamed and afraid, and never told anyone about it. Unsurprisingly, my brother and I never did manage to have a good relationship. He died young in an accident, long before I started my transition. I think if he had lived to see it, he would have been appalled. Certainly he was outraged to the point of violence when I started dating women.

On one memorable occasion I visited my parents with the woman I was then living with (my first female lover). My brother came home, drunk, and attacked my lover. He was a strong man, and he had to be pulled off by four people. I am unfortunately not a large person, and could not do much to help. I picked up a glass ashtray and tried to bash him over the head with it, but failed. At that point he had my lover on her back and was trying to throttle her. That was the only time my mother ever called the police on one of her own children. I can still remember her hands and voice shaking as she called them. My brother then fled the house, ending the attack. We never visited my parents again while my brother was still alive and living with my parents – about another four years.

But to return to my childhood: after the event with the boys throwing stones at me, I mainly kept to myself, spending time with my endless succession of bikes and dogs. I always had a beloved dog and a beloved bike, and those were usually enough for me. I did get lonely from time to time, though.

I remember one day resolving to try and play with the girls in the neighborhood. I must have been really desperate. I walked self-consciously down the driveway of Lynda, who was the girl pack leader in our neighborhood. Every girl in the neighborhood was there. They all looked up at me as I walked tentatively towards them. Their eyes were distrusting and skeptical.

"Can I play too?" I asked.

They looked me up and down. They were playing House, which was a game in which each girl pretended to be a member of the family.

At last, Lynda said grudgingly, "All right, you can be the brother."

I think I only played for about five minutes, but it felt like a lifetime. My cheeks were burning and my palms were sweating. I felt so deeply humiliated to be playing such an obviously "girl" game, with a whole group of girls who I experienced as both strange and intimidating. It dawned on me that I could not pull this off. I could not be one of them. I suddenly took off at a run, and never looked back. I fetched my bike and my dog and headed for the bush, my cheeks still burning with the shame of it.

I tried again to play with the boys. We played stingers, a game in which a boy is tagged by having a small, hard ball thrown at him. After repeatedly being singled out for very hard-thrown balls, I gave up and retreated again. I am fair skinned, and I was badly bruised by that game. I can still see the malicious venom in the eyes of some of the boys as they hurled that ball at me. It was like they had been given a license to attack the freak, and they took full advantage of it.

Unable to be with the girls or the boys, I spent my childhood in a solitary way. At school I did not join the girls in their skipping or the boys in their ball games. Skipping did not even occur to me as a possibility, and the boys would not let me join their games. Luckily I was a reader, and was able to lose myself in Superman and Batman comics, and an endless succession of boy's fiction. I loved the *Just William* books, and read them all at least twice. And I loved the *Billy Bunter* books almost as much. In my head and in my fantasies

I was a boy. I trudged miles to borrow and buy the comics and books that created a boy universe for me, and I managed to be absorbed and happy quite a lot of the time. But from the perspective of other people, I must have seemed like a somewhat pathetic little girl.

It all came to a screeching halt when I was twelve. To add insult to injury, fate decreed that I would mature early, and I was the first person in my class to develop breasts. I resolutely ignored them. I continued to wear boy's clothes and to work on developing my muscles – a hopeless endeavor, as all of my biology was working against me. Instead of growing the biceps I craved, I grew conspicuous bumps on my chest. I vividly remember one day at school, standing in the stairwell near Steve, a class mate. He was an unusually well-muscled boy, and he would not-too-subtly adopt poses that showed his muscles off to best advantage. I gazed at him, with his angular lines and sharply defined muscles in his shorts and short sleeves, and felt almost overcome by misery. He was the boy I wanted to be, and I had no way of becoming him.

One day my mother faced me nervously but squarely and told me that it was time to start "behaving like a girl." Then she produced three things she had just bought for me: two brightly colored dresses, and a white bra. The dresses were decorated with rows of frilly white lace. I felt like the sky had fallen down on me.

I realize now that I had been ignoring reality. I had somehow thought that if I just kept living as a boy, I would miraculously become a man. But instead I was becoming a woman. Nature was relentless, and every sign was clear. I was becoming a woman, and everyone could see it. My mother made me put on the bra and one of the dresses, and took me to the library.

At the library, we bumped into a boy from my class, Leo. I remember the enormous shame I felt. Now, he would know that I was a girl, not a boy. Of course, Leo was not surprised in any way. He had known all along that I was a girl, and therefore he was completely unsurprised to see me in a dress. I felt sick as I realized that I had not been fooling anyone. My male self-image in my head was so strong that I had really believed that everyone else saw me as I saw myself – as a boy.

That was the beginning of a painful, shameful descent into reality. At that time, I had never heard of gender reassignment, and I assumed that I was doomed to spend my life pretending to be the girl that everyone believed I was. I grew into womanhood in that way, ashamed, confused, and occasionally suicidal. At one point I put on a large amount of weight. Looking back, I think it was a way to hide myself. (Although it was also partly my own biology.)

After becoming an adult, I spent about ten years drinking a lot of alcohol, which I guess was a way to numb myself. Then for another twenty years I just focused on my career and my relationships (with women), and tried to forget who I was.

Years later, I finally learned that there were ways to deal with the dissonance between my female designation and my feeling of being male. I learned that I could take steps to make my gender expression as male as possible, so as to alleviate the uncomfortable and sometimes unbearable dissonance between how I felt and how people perceived me. Like many other people in this predicament, I defied society and began dressing and acting in the masculine way that seemed natural to me. This bought me to a situation of living on the border of the gender binary.

Living on the Border of the Gender Binary

There are some women who appear quite masculine, but who are in fact quite happy with being designated as women, and who identify as belonging to the female gender. These women will almost invariably be punished by society for their gender expression, but they do not want to change their gender designation. This book is not about them. However, by their very existence, these women contest the primacy of the gender binary – the social idea that everyone has to fit neatly into male or female categories.

Feminist theorists such as Butler and Halberstam have critiqued this social requirement, arguing that gender expression is something most people subconsciously choose to enact each and every day. They describe society's demand that people fit into the category of either male or female as a "binary prescription." There are people who oppose this rigid prescription. Some of them describe themselves as gender queer, and live their lives in such a way as to actively undermine this binary prescription. Such people are incredibly brave, and have my utmost respect.

CROSSING OVER THE BORDER OF THE GENDER BINARY

I tried to be one of those people for a long time, living on the border of the gender binary. I looked and behaved like a man, but accepted being designated as female. My name was androgynous. However, I could not sustain it for more than a few years. I just got so tired of being regarded as a weird social misfit.

One particularly unpleasant experience at that time was starting a new job. I could tell throughout the interview process that they were not sure of my gender. To their credit, they hired me for my qualifications, and ignored the very unusual fact that they were not sure if they were hiring a man or a woman. On my first day I had to produce my identity documents, and they were able to tell that I was designated female. This resulted in a flurry of whispered conversations on the peripheries of my consciousness – I knew that everyone was being told that I was in fact female. I was then introduced to the various members of staff, and the supervisor who was introducing me kept saying things like, "This is our new team member, **she** is joining us today." I think he was trying to be kind, but I cringed every time he said it.

In retrospect, I should have been braver. At that point in my life I was presenting as so male that it would have been easier and wiser to have had a word with the boss and requested to be treated as male. But I didn't have the courage to do that, and so I endured years in a job where I looked male but was treated as female. (My wife says it was not surprising I did not have the courage, as I was at a very vulnerable stage of my life.) As I had quite a lot of contact with people from other businesses, those few years were really tough. I was constantly aware of being the subject of whispered explanations. It was a very white-collar job, and everyone was scrupulously polite about it. No one ever mentioned the enormous elephant in the room. But it was still enormously uncomfortable for me.

Living on the border of the gender binary is incredibly tough. Some brave souls manage to do it permanently. Many of them don't identify as transgendered, simply as gender queer. However, this book is not about those brave souls; it is about people who choose to move from one side to the other side of the gender binary. Specifically, it is about female-bodied people who choose to move to the male side of the gender binary – FTMs.

Some FTMs are fortunate enough to be able to take dramatic steps to bring their outward presentation into line with the way they feel (their gender identity as men). This book is largely about these people: FTMs such as me who are able to transition to a much more male presentation, and finally to be accepted by most or all of the world as male. The steps we take may include having hormone treatment, undergoing various surgeries, having a legal name change, changing identity documents, adopting masculine haircuts, and dressing in male-designated clothing. FTMs like me believe that we are in fact men, but that our bodies simply don't reflect that reality, and therefore we work to change our bodies and presentation.

WHAT MAKES US FTM?

There are a variety of theories about what makes us FTM. No one is quite sure how many people are transgendered. Some estimates put it as high as 1.5 per cent of the population, but there is no way of being certain, due to the fact that most people hide this condition, to avoid being rejected, beaten, or killed.

It's my belief that it starts in the womb, when the brain is masculinized but the body is feminized, due to a mistake in the sequence of hormonal "baths" that the fetus is exposed to. Interestingly, it has in fact been proven by scientists that one can deliberately *create* FTM monkeys by manipulating prenatal hormones.

Robert Goy and his co-researchers in the mid 1980s showed that it was possible to masculinize female monkeys by exposing them to the male hormone androgen prior to birth (Wallen). This resulted in the birth of biologically female monkeys that behaved exactly like male monkeys throughout their lives. The researchers argued that this could be an explanation for the human phenomenon of transsexualism. Another prominent researcher and theorist in this field, Dr. Milton Diamond, put it this way:

> The brain and the genitals can be differentiated and develop independently … [I]t's conclusive for monkeys. And I happen to think, with this matter, that we can extrapolate to humans. (Kotula, 53)

Similar conditions to those that the researchers artificially set up occur naturally when pregnant humans are exposed to stress, and it has been noted that many of the babies that were in vitro during the London Blitz subsequently turned out to be transgendered.

This theory fits the way I have experienced my life. My body was unequivocally female, but my brain has always been entirely convinced that I am male. This conviction remained absolutely intact despite decades of social pressure from my family and my society. This amount of societal pressure should have been irresistible, yet I resisted it. This seems to be the common thread with FTMs: we believe that we have a male gender (mind) but a female sex (body), and therefore we are usually uncomfortable with being classified as members of the female gender. And no amount of social pressure can convince us otherwise.

Unfortunately, this contradictory state of affairs is currently defined as a Gender Identity Disorder (GID).

GENDER IDENTITY DISORDER (GID)

Gender identity Disorder (GID) is currently classified as a psychiatric disorder in the DSM-IV TR. The DSM is the *Diagnostic and Statistical Manual of Mental Disorders* published by the American Psychiatric Association. The IV TR version was published in 2000).

"In 1994, the DSM-IV committee replaced the diagnosis of Transsexualism with Gender Identity Disorder. Depending on their age, those with a strong and persistent cross-gender identification and a persistent discomfort with his or her sex or a sense of inappropriateness in the gender role of that sex were to be diagnosed as Gender Identity Disorder of Childhood (302.6), Adolescence, or Adulthood (302.85)."
(Harry Benjamin Standards of Care)

The diagnosis of Gender Identity Disorder is applied to people who experience significant gender dysphoria, that is, discontent with the sex they were assigned at birth and/or the gender roles associated with that sex. In some countries, being diagnosed as having this "disorder" opens the door to the approved treatments for this disorder.

For example, in most of Canada, hormonal treatment and some (but not all) surgical interventions are covered by provincial health plans. In the USA, as of December 2014, the states of California, Colorado, Connecticut, Illinois, Massachusetts, Oregon, Vermont, and Washington required health insurance companies to cover transition costs for people diagnosed with gender dysphoria. In that same month, New York Governor Andrew M. Cuomo warned insurance companies that they would no longer be allowed to deny gender reassignment surgery or other treatment to change a person's gender, like hormone therapy, if a doctor had deemed that treatment to be medically necessary.

The next version of the DSM will most likely replace the category Gender identity Disorder (GID) with "gender dysphoria," which is a much less loaded term, as it simply describes how we feel, rather than designating our feelings as a disorder. This will be a definite improvement. I personally take offence that my mental state is defined as disordered.

A person with gender dysphoria is transgendered, that is, their gender identity does not match their assigned (biological) sex. Such people are also termed transsexual, as this means pretty much exactly the same thing. I cannot see a difference, and personally I identify as both transgendered and transsexual, depending on which day of the week it is. However, some people reserve the word transsexual for those who have undergone surgeries.

How do FTMs Identify Ourselves?

There is a wide range of ways that FTMs define ourselves. We may call ourselves trans guys or transmen or FTMs or trannies, or just simply "men."

Living Stealth

Some men choose to go stealth: to go through the transition and then let everyone around them assume that they have always lived as men. Some men go to new cities or countries or continents to achieve this. There are some excellent reasons to go stealth, notably to avoid being murdered. Transgendered people are still sometimes attacked and even murdered, because for some reason, some people really hate us. Apparently we threaten something deep within them, and they cope with this by attacking us. A notable example is Brandon Teena, who was raped and murdered when his "friends" realized he was biologically female.

On a less brutal note, being stealth about the fact that we were previously identified as woman can protect us from discrimination, which may help us get jobs and generally survive financially. As of this time, the vast majority of people on our planet are not protected from discrimination on the grounds of gender identity.

Personally, I am totally stealth (except that people I have known for longer than fourteen years know that I was previously designated female). I have not gone to the lengths of changing countries, but I did change jobs so that I could start fresh in a company where people perceived me only as a man. This was the right path for me. I started my transition while employed, and I found it incredibly stressful. People kept forgetting to call me "he," and on one notable occasion someone in a meeting called me "Madam Chairwoman," causing me to cringe. Everyone seemed to feel awkward all the time, and I knew that some people saw me as a freak, even though they weren't allowed to say so. Other people were amazingly supportive, yet still saw me as a woman.

In particular, I had problems with the washrooms. I am one of those people who need to go frequently, and I no longer felt comfortable in the women's washroom. However, I could not imagine going into the men's room with men who had known me as a woman for years. Fortunately, there was one gender-neutral washroom in the building, for people with disabilities, and that saved me. I remember one day it was out of order for several hours, and I very nearly exploded! I eventually went and told the handyman that there was a disabled person in the building who was in dire need. I did not tell him that the person was me, and that my "disability" was that no one took me seriously as a man.

IDENTIFYING AS ONE OF THE MEN AT WORK

Starting a new job as a man felt like having an enormous psychological weight removed from me. Everyone, absolutely everyone, calls me "he." No one ever makes a mistake, because no one has ever known me as anything but male. There is no problem in the washroom. Other men talk to me in the washroom in a casual way (contrary to popular belief among women, men do actually talk to each other in washrooms, as long as they know each other). Also contrary to popular belief, I have never once heard another man at work talk disrespectfully about women in general, or about his wife in particular. When wives are mentioned, it is invariably in a positive way. It seems to me that, like me, most men are just amazed and proud that someone would actually marry them.

Having previously been in the workplace as a woman, it

is interesting to now work as a man. I have formed the kind of casual and superficial friendships with other men that are expected in the workplace. I talk to other men about subjects of common interest, such as bikes and wives.

Along the way, I have learned some things I never expected. For example, men talk to each other about diets and weight, just as women do. But we never do it when women are around! However, I have never yet had a discussion with any of the men at the office about feelings of any kind (apart from the generic "thank God it's Friday" kind of thing). The only problems I ever discuss with men at the office are related to financial or work pressures, or the weather. I am fortunate that I work with so many geeks that my complete lack of interest in organized sports is not even noticed. In fact, after several years of living as a man, that particular lack of knowledge has never been a problem. But that is probably because most of the men I work with are more interested in Batman than baseball.

I do find that I have a few really good relationships with women at the office. I am close to a few women at the office, while all my relationships with men at the office are superficial at best. I don't know if those women that I am close to find this odd. I don't know if they think of me as a strange man, or even if they wonder whether I am transgendered. But as long as they keep unfailingly calling me "he," I can deal with the uncertainty. I have asked friends who know me well what they think – they think that no one at work ever suspects my past. As they say, people see what they want to see. Once you reach a certain point on your transition journey, people see you as male, and they don't let minor details (such as hand size) distract them.

Interestingly, I have earned about 20% more since transitioning, even though I now have a less demanding job. Apparently, gender discrimination in the workplace is alive and well. Now it is working for me instead of against me, but that does not make it right.

I am able to be stealth because I have had the material resources (and medical coverage) to create a male chest and to be on testosterone (T) long enough to be reasonably hairy, appear male, have a reasonably deep voice, and to have very obvious male-pattern baldness. However, I am very short and have small hands. I was small compared to average women, so I am tiny compared to average men. In fact, my small size was a big factor that delayed me starting transition. Because of my small size, I can never be completely certain that I will not be detected. I sometimes find myself in situations where I keep my hands under the table, so as not to draw attention to my most obviously non-male characteristic. Or I keep my gloves on long after others have taken theirs off. A lot of transmen are in this position. It helps to remember that height and hand size varies tremendously even among bio men. And it really helps to go on vacation to Mexico, where I am average height for a man!

There are some very brave and committed people who choose to affirm publicly and vocally that they are transmen, because they feel that this provides a positive role model for people who are struggling with gender dysphoria and are afraid to do something about it. I admire these men very much, but I am not personally able to do that. I just want to blend.

However, I believe that there is no right way to identify yourself: it comes down to what you feel comfortable with, what you believe in, and what you are able to achieve. We are all trying to be the best people we can be, but we all have different abilities and limitations. I have to admit that I feel very comfortable when I am with people who have never known me as anything but a man, because I can just blend in and feel "average" and "normal." This is a new thing in my life: I have lived for decades feeling like a misfit, feeling unable to be "one of the girls" because I just wasn't one of them. The joy of being able to fit in and just be "one of the guys" is indescribable.

On the other hand, my life will always be full of people who knew me when I was still socially identified as female. Going stealth all of the time is simply not an option for me, so for some people, I will always be a transman, not just one of the guys. And for some people, notably my mother, I will always be a woman.

How I Changed My Gender ...

I admit that sometimes I think I would just like to move to a different country where no one has ever known me, so that I don't have to deal with people who persistently think of me as female. But I have a lot of very beloved friends who fit into that category, and I would hate to lose them. At the same time, it is terribly undermining and depressing, after all these years of transition, to be at a social gathering and have someone accidentally call me "she." At such times I just want to walk away from decades of friendships and start all over again.

To some extent other people define us, and to some extent we define ourselves. Deciding to gender transition is a gigantic, confident step that says:

"I choose to define who I am, regardless of how the entire world has defined me for the whole of my life up to now – and regardless of how the world defines me in the future."

I think that's a tremendously courageous step to take. Beyond that, how you deal with it and what you call yourself is up to you. Just bear in mind that some people will always see you as female, even if you lose all your hair and grow a ten-inch beard. Depressing but true. A wise friend once counseled me not to take offence at this, and to remember that it is just hard for some people to shift their mental picture.

GENDER IDENTITY AND SEXUAL ORIENTATION

Gender identity is how we feel about our gender, and sexual orientation is who we feel sexually attracted to. The connection between these two is as varied as human nature. I have written more about this later in this book. For now, suffice it to say that becoming a man in society does not necessarily mean that one will want to have sex with a woman. Some transmen are attracted to men, some to women, some to both, and some to neither.

A transman who is attracted to men is defined as gay, regardless of the fact that he was born with female genitalia, and may still have them. The point is that he is attracted to people who have the same gender expression as he does. Based on the same logic, a transman who is attracted to women is defined as straight.

Of course, as those of us who live in the gender twilight zone know, nothing is simple. For example, if one member of a lesbian couple transitions to male, his partner does not magically become straight at the moment that her partner becomes male. But she is now a woman living with a man, so it becomes difficult (or impossible) for her to be perceived by society as a lesbian. It may also be deeply confusing and disturbing for her, as she struggles to internalize what this means about her own sexual orientation. Similarly, a man living with a woman who becomes a man does not magically become gay overnight. And he is likely to find it very stressful when his wife becomes his husband. All of this can be very difficult, and has caused many relationships to end. There is a huge need for organizations to support such people, but at this time they are few and far between.

My own partner has gone through difficult times with my transition. When we met she was living as a straight woman, married to a non-trans man. She had been living as straight for her entire life (more than forty years at that time). We fell in love and she left her husband to be with me. She then had to come out to all her friends and family as a lesbian, which was of course very traumatic for her and for them. A few years later, I told her I was transitioning. This made her feel very confused about her own orientation and about how to define herself. It made her feel awkward around the people she had come out to. Should she now reverse her announcement about being a lesbian? And as she said to me on one memorable occasion, when she married me, she had not signed up to be with a man.

We did resolve the issue after some time. She accepted my argument that we don't need to be neatly labeled; we can just be who we are. And also that we will always be a gender queer couple; it is just that now we are gender queer in a different way. She says that what it comes down to for her is that she loves me and wants me to be happy. She understands that living as an intensely masculine "woman" was becoming more and more unbearable for me. She understands that it was very hard for me to be perceived as a gender freak at my place of work. And she knows that I am still the same person, only a much happier person. She has become a rock of support, and always introduces me as her husband. At first she would sometimes accidentally refer to me as "she," but she doesn't do that anymore. I will always be grateful to her for allowing me to become myself, even at the cost of having to reevaluate and somewhat redefine her own identity. In doing this, she has shown true love and respect for who I am, and for what I need to be happy.

What is the Prescribed Medical Treatment if You Are FTM?

As noted above, people who are FTM may be diagnosed as having gender identity disorder, which is perceived as a mental illness. While it was distasteful to me be diagnosed as being mentally ill, it did have the positive result that it opened the door to medical treatment. I had to have an interview with three psychiatrists to confirm my GID diagnosis. I told them that I found it very odd that I was sitting there trying to prove to them that I was mentally ill. They agreed that it was a strange situation, but that it was necessary for me to get access to medical treatment.

Some people speculate that the system works like this so that physicians will not get sued for treating us. If for example a female-bodied person complained that testosterone had deepened their voice and had now decided this was negatively impacting his or her job prospects, he or she could not sue their doctor if they had a GID diagnosis. The doctor would simply argue that he had followed the approved medical protocols and treatment for an individual diagnosed with a gender identity disorder.

In any event, once diagnosed, you may be able to access the recommended medical interventions. Many FTMs very desperately want medical assistance to change our bodies to look more like the male gender we believe we belong to. Medical treatment usually comprises hormone therapy (testosterone) and various surgeries, all intended to masculinize the body. These are usually accompanied by counseling in order to assist us to make such a huge transition (and to keep checking that we really need and want this treatment).

The Harry Benjamin Standards of Care define in great detail the standards that physicians must adhere to in diagnosing and treating GID. These can be easily found on the Internet.

Chapter 2: Hormone Therapy – The Magic of Testosterone

Testosterone: Your First Step to Manhood!

For most people the first step towards changing gender is hormone therapy. In the case of FTMs, testosterone therapy is used to bring about the desired masculinization. In the FTM community, testosterone is commonly referred to as T. Once you start testosterone, it will cause enormous changes in your body and mind. An important caveat is that many of these changes are irreversible – if you stop taking testosterone, some of the physical changes will not go away. And if you are one of the tiny minority that changes their mind about transitioning, you may not be happy with these changes in the long term.

I do know someone who did this. She got halfway through a transition when she was 21, and for the 33 years since then, she has had to live as a woman who has a very deep voice and no breasts. She has never had children, so it is possible that the testosterone permanently destroyed her fertility as well. To be fair, she was never the most stable person. Mistakes of this kind are very uncommon.

But clearly, you need to be 100% sure that you want to transition before you start hormone therapy. That's why I personally believe it's not a bad thing that all jurisdictions require some professional counseling before giving the go-ahead for people – even sane, mature, intelligent adults – to transition gender.

I still remember vividly the day I got my first prescription for testosterone – it was like I had been given the key to start my incredible journey to maleness. It was magical. It is like this for many of us. Within days of my first testosterone shot I started to change. My voice cracked and broke within a month. People kept asking me if I had a cold! Now of course everyone is used to my voice, and my wife laughs out loud when we see a video of me pre-T, with my old, girlish voice! After my very first shot, I never had another period again, ever (joy!). This is unusual – most people still have one or two periods before they finally go away. It may be that mine stopped sooner because I was already in my forties. The happy side effect of all this was that I completed avoided menopause (something that makes my wife very jealous, as her menopause dragged on for the best part of a decade).

The physical changes to my appearance (facial features, fat distribution, muscle distribution) were much, much slower – in fact, they kind of snuck up on me. However, there is no doubt that the first shot of testosterone into my thigh muscle was the first step on my journey to becoming the man I was always meant to be. It was the beginning of a long, arduous journey to make the outside me match the inside me. I have now gone far enough on that journey that I feel comfortable in my skin and in the world – for the first time in my life.

How I Got Testosterone

To get my testosterone, I had to go through several sessions of counseling with an approved gender counselor. She was sure from the first minute that I was the real deal, but we both knew that we had to go through the process. Unfortunately, to qualify for hormone therapy in most places, you need to be diagnosed as having Gender Identity Disorder.

This diagnosis also comes with a whole lot of assumptions about us. Most significantly, many psychiatrists are convinced that genuine FTMs are attracted only to women (reflecting a heterosexist perception of the world, in which changing the sex of the patient would restore the heteronormative standard). Because of this, presenting oneself as attracted to men could reduce one's chances of being classified as having Gender Identity Disorder, and thereby close the door to the option of treatment with testosterone and surgeries. I have met many transmen who have pretended to be solely attracted to women in order to "please" their therapist and thus get the desired treatment.

Moreover, people often have to prove that they have Gender Identity Disorder more than once. For example, I had to prove to a counselor that I had Gender Identity Disorder in order to qualify for testosterone; years later I had to appear before two psychiatrists to convince them that I had Gender Identity Disorder in order to get medical coverage for my double mastectomy. I told the two psychiatrists that I found it a bit bizarre that I was actually trying to prove that I was mentally ill; they agreed with me that it was bizarre, but reminded me that the system requires a diagnosis in order to prescribe a treatment.

I understand that, but still I would prefer that Gender Identity Disorder be classified as a physical condition, caused by prenatal hormones. To me the advantage of perceiving Gender Identity Disorder in this way is that it puts the emphasis on a physical condition over which I have no control, rather than saying I have a mental disorder. One might argue that people also don't have control over mental disorders. However, there is a big stigma attached to mental health issues that can significantly impact quality of life, self-esteem, and career opportunities. Moreover, many mental health professionals tend to assume that if a person has one mental heath disorder, they are likely to have others. Admittedly symptoms like depression and anxiety are common in transsexuals, but that is surely a result of living in a hostile society, rather than a result of inherent mental health issues.

In any event, the first step in your journey is to get someone to say you have a mental disorder called Gender Identity Disorder, which you then take to your doctor, who then needs to follow the Harry Benjamin Standards of Care and prescribe testosterone for you.

WAYS TO TAKE TESTOSTERONE

Testosterone can be administered in various ways:
- intramuscular injection into one of the large muscles, usually the thigh or the buttock;
- applying a gel every day;
- having a transdermal implant placed under the skin, usually the abdomen or buttocks; or

- an oral tablet (this is not recommended because of liver toxicity).

The gel has to be applied daily, and most people (including endocrinologists I have consulted) agree that it is less effective in masculinization than injections. Injections are usually taken once a week or every second week. My endocrinologist swears it makes no difference, so I inject every two weeks. However, many people believe that a weekly dose keeps one's levels more stable. Experiment to see what works for you. If you listen carefully to your body, you will know. For myself, I know that I am overdue for my testosterone if I become very angry, irritable, and moody.

Your choices of injection sites are thigh and glute (the two biggest muscles). The advantage of the glute is that it is such a big muscle that I have never experienced any pain or bruising post-injection in that site. The disadvantage of the glute as an injection site is that unless you are an Olympic gymnast, it is really hard to inject your own glute. The disadvantage of the thigh as an injection site is that one can occasionally experience bruising in this site; I have had several days when I have been limping due to having my shot the previous day. On the other hand, most of us have a choice of two thighs, so it is possible to rotate.

Bear in mind that testosterone is a thick, viscous liquid and it can be quite hard to depress the needle, especially if you use a thin needle. Personally I find it fairly easy to inject my own thigh, and completely impossible to inject my own glute – I can scarcely twist my arm that much, let alone apply strong pressure with my thumb once in that position.

What I do is draw up the testosterone with a thick needle so that it is quite easy to draw it up, and then switch over to a thin needle for the injection. Some people think that the thin needle does not go deep enough, but I have used it for fourteen years and it has delivered the testosterone to my system just fine. And a thin needle has the major advantage that it is much less painful than a thick needle. The disadvantage is that because it is being administered via a very thin needle, it is all the more difficult to push the testosterone through.

Whether you do your own injections or get someone to do them for you comes down to personal preference. Personally I had my first shot done by my doctor, who showed me how to do it, and thereafter I did it myself. I found it pretty easy, and being so experienced with injecting came in handy when one of my children needed regular injections. Nowadays my wife usually injects my glute, as I was having increasingly frequent problems with bruising on my thighs.

Obviously if you can learn to do your own shot it makes it more convenient. But some people choose to go to a medical clinic to have it done. I know men who spend half a day once a week to travel to a clinic to have a shot. I would hate to do that, but if you really can't stand the idea of injecting yourself, that may be an option for you.

One thing to bear in mind is that the injection really does not hurt much, if at all. It is counter-intuitive to stick a sharp needle into your own body, but because the needle is so tiny, it scarcely hurts at all. Sometimes when my wife does my shots, I don't even know she's done it until she tells me it's done.

MEDICAL SUPERVISION OF TESTOSTERONE TREATMENT

It is absolutely essential that you take testosterone under medical supervision. It has powerful impacts on your body, and not all of them are good. Like all medications, it may have a range of side effects. And like most medications, monitoring is necessary to achieve and maintain the correct dosage – in this case, a dosage that achieves the desired masculinization, without putting too much strain on your body or causing negative side effects.

Moreover, testosterone places a load on your kidneys, which have to process the medication. Therefore, it is essential to have regular blood work to check your kidney function. Liver function must also be carefully monitored.

When I started on T, my doctor had no idea what was necessary. As a result, I was not properly monitored, and developed one or two medical complications that were not pleasant. Now I am under the care of a skilled endocrinologist, who knows what he is doing, and who monitors me carefully by doing thorough blood work every six months. The tests he does include the following, which are standard for all FTMs on testosterone:

- Hemoglobin/Hematocrit
- Liver Function Panel (or ALT)
- Lipid Panel
- Glucose or Hgb A1C

You should have at least this much monitoring if you are on testosterone. And before you even start, it is recommended that you get baseline testing for all of the following:

- Weight and Blood Pressure
- Fasting Lipid Profile
- Fasting Glucose or Hgb A1C
- If sexually active with men, pregnancy test (if positive, testosterone therapy is absolutely contraindicated until the pregnancy is completed or terminated)
- Kidney Function (with or without urinalysis)
- Liver Function Panel (or ALT)
- Hormonal or Genetic Studies – possibly including estradiol, testosterone, prolactin, cosyntropin stimulation test, and LH (if indicated by history and physical)
- PAP and STD Screening (if not recently performed and/or if indicated by history and physical)

(Gorton et al.)

If you are under the care of a doctor who does not know the requirements for monitoring people on testosterone, try giving him or her this excellent document: Gorton et al., *Medical Therapy and Health Maintenance for Transgender Men: A Guide For Health Care Providers* (available on the Internet). You could try sending your doctor a link or providing a physical copy. Of course, not all doctors are open to being educated by their patients, but the fact that this document was written by a medical doctor might carry some weight. If that fails, insist on a referral to an endocrinologist who is trans friendly and who will be able to monitor you correctly.

As mentioned above, in my early years on testosterone, I had a doctor who knew little about trans needs (I was her first trans patient). I did not know enough to ask for a referral to an endocrinologist. As a result, I ended up with polycythemia, a disease state in which the proportion of blood volume that is occupied by red blood cells increases. My testosterone dosage was too high, and that had caused the problem. It's been reversed now, but I do have permanent skin damage from it (burst capillaries just under the skin). And I was lucky, because it could have been a lot more serious. I know of people who have developed life-threatening nose bleeds because they had polycythemia and did not realize it. I now protect myself against polycythemia with regular blood donations – and of course proper medical monitoring.

TESTOSTERONE AND RISK OF DISEASES

There is no definitive research as to whether taking testosterone increases your risk of cardiovascular disease. However, some things are known. Testosterone may cause negative changes in your lipid profile, which is a known risk factor for cardiovascular disease. This happened with me, and consequently I am on a statin drug to keep my lipids in a healthy range. At one point this scared me so much that I stopped taking testosterone for a while. But then my endocrinologist pointed out that half the human race manages to have high testosterone levels and survives, and so I went back on it. I just have to make a point of eating well and getting plenty of exercise. During the nine months I was off testosterone, I put on a lot of weight and felt cold all the time. I have also put on weight when I accidentally let my testosterone levels get too low. It's a constant balancing act, emphasizing again the need for careful medical monitoring.

Androgen therapy tends to decrease overall body fat, but redistributes fat toward the typical male pattern of abdominal obesity, which is associated with higher cardiovascular risk than fat on the buttocks and hips. It also causes an increase in visceral fat mass, and this is a known risk factor for cardiovascular disease. Testosterone therapy is also associated with an increase in plasma homocysteine, which is a known risk factor for cardiovascular disease. In some people testosterone may cause weight gain and decreased insulin sensitivity. This can be a problem, especially if one is already predisposed toward Type II diabetes. I am in this category, and my father died from diabetes. However, my doctor says I have successfully prevented myself from developing Type II diabetes because of my healthy diet and high exercise levels (Gorton et al.).

On the plus side, the medical consensus seems to be that a transman is at no greater risk for cardiovascular disease than a bio man of the same age. And of course, the fact that one feels happier must surely have a positive impact on health.

Testosterone may put you at higher risk of several diseases, or make them worse if you already have them. If you are worried about any of the following, you should talk to your doctor. You probably won't be forced to stop testosterone, but you will be able to access treatment. These are the diseases/syndromes:

- Type 2 diabetes
- Liver disease
- High blood pressure
- High cholesterol
- Heart disease
- Migraine headaches
- Sleep apnea
- Epilepsy

(Gorton et al.)

WHAT TESTOSTERONE WILL DO FOR YOU: PHYSICAL AND EMOTIONAL CHANGES

Testosterone causes some permanent, irreversible changes, and some changes that will disappear if you stop using testosterone. These are the reversible changes:

- Muscle and strength development
- Increased energy in some
- Increased libido
- Redistribution of body fat

- Cessation of ovulation and menstruation
- Increased sweat
- Changes in body odor
- Veins become more prominent
- Coarsening of skin
- Acne and oily skin in some
- Elevated blood lipids (cholesterol and triglycerides)
- Increased red blood cell count

These are the irreversible changes:
- Deepening of the voice
- Enlargement of the clitoris
- Developing male pattern baldness

Increase in facial and body hair is said to be irreversible, but when I stopped taking testosterone the hair on my stomach disappeared after a few months, and my facial hair also stopped growing eventually. My legs stayed very hairy, though. When I went back on testosterone, all of my body and facial hair very quickly grew back.

CHANGES IN LIBIDO

All people have both estrogen and testosterone in their bodies. However, the proportions and amounts are very different in men and women. Testosterone is responsible in large part for everybody's sex drive, but the average man has 32 times as much testosterone in his body as the average woman. I think it would be fair to say that one's sex drive increases by at least 32 times as much when one starts injecting testosterone. Personally, I started understanding why men are often accused of thinking about sex all the time.

This is one of the reversible changes – if you stop taking testosterone, your sex drive will return to pre-testosterone levels. I know, because I was on testosterone for several years, stopped for nine months, and then went back on testosterone. The difference each time was like night and day. As one trans man described it, being on testosterone makes you feel a little like you have been sexually asleep all your life until then.

For me it felt as if my sex drive went from about 10 to

100 in a matter of weeks. Be prepared for this. It is a very big change, and can be disturbing for some. Personally I enjoy the way my sex drive has been increased by testosterone.

Many transmen, myself included, develop a new understanding of non-trans men once they go on testosterone. Suddenly it makes sense that there is so much porn in the world. Arguments against porn start to seem ridiculous, because you begin to understand that it is well nigh impossible to expect the average man to live without it. And you understand why teenage boys are so singularly obsessed with sex, once you share that fixation yourself!

You will look at the world differently once you have high levels of testosterone in your body. You will watch TV and movies differently. You will notice things you have never noticed before – almost all of them sexual things, such as people's bodies. Some transmen find themselves regarding everybody in a sexual light – that is, while they may only have been interested in women before, they now find both men and women attractive and sexually interesting.

You may find that you have to fight with yourself not to waste too many hours of the day on sexual fantasies – a struggle that many bio men before you have experienced!

Voice Changes

Testosterone will increase the size of your larynx and thereby change your voice. Many of us notice changes and deepening within a few weeks of starting testosterone – I certainly did. This change is irreversible. So if you sing in a choir, expect some changes in your life. At the same time, many of us never develop voices that are quite as deep as bio men. I find that when I am on the phone with strangers, they will sometimes think I am female. This never happens face-to-face, and I don't think people notice my voice much at all when I am physically present. After all, bio males also have a wide variety in the depth of their voices.

Also, people tend to construct reality based on what they see. If a bearded male-looking person is talking to them, they perceive a man, and they are unlikely to notice that his voice is a little on the high side. Their brain has constructed that person as a man, based on visible clues such as hairstyle, beard, and clothing. With that construction in their heads, their brain seems to make the entire picture coherent.

IMPACT OF TESTOSTERONE ON MENSTRUAL PERIODS AND FERTILITY

Obviously, once you are on testosterone your entire biological cycle is tremendously impacted. Personally I never had another period after my first shot of testosterone, so I experienced a kind of instant menopause, without any negative symptoms (causing my wife to envy me intensely, as her menopause lasted about ten years and included every possible negative symptom). Other men don't see a cessation of their periods until they have been on testosterone for a few weeks to a few months. However, providing your dosage is correct, they definitely will stop.

Of course, testosterone will put an end to your fertility, for at least as long as you are on it. Note that this does not happen instantly, so if have sex with men, don't think you have taken a miraculous contraceptive after you have had your first shot of testosterone. For a variable length of time after beginning testosterone, it remains possible to become pregnant.

There was the famous case of Thomas Beatie from Oregon, a transman on testosterone who was fully masculinized, who stopped taking testosterone for a period of time so as to become pregnant and carry a baby girl to term in 2008 – thus becoming the first man to have a baby. Since then, a German trans man has given birth to a baby boy, in 2013.

Both these pregnant men faced difficulties and discrimination. The German man even had difficulty getting medical care. This seems to me to be doing things the hard way: if you plan to have a baby, it would be much easier to do it before starting testosterone, or to freeze some eggs that could later be carried by a surrogate mother. However, of course the decision or desire to have a baby may come later in life, and everyone has the right to try to actualize his or her needs when it is possible and does not cause any harm to anybody else.

There has been little research on the impact of testosterone on fertility. But the long-term effect of testosterone is atrophy of the uterus and ovaries, resulting in sterility.

GENITAL CHANGES

Most people experience quite significant changes to the vagina once they are taking testosterone. It may become smaller, the walls may become thinner, and lubrication may be significantly reduced. For some men these changes are so minor that they are not noticed.

One thing almost every trans man will experience is significant clitoral growth. This is also an irreversible change – it will not shrink back to pre-testosterone size if you stop. On the other hand, I have never yet met anyone, transman or woman, who said, "I wish my clitoris was smaller!"

As your clitoris grows you will become increasingly aware that the clitoris and the penis are essentially the same organs. The difference is that in bio males, hormones in the womb cause the clitoris to develop into a penis. Hence, as your clitoris grows it becomes more recognizably a small penis. I nurture a hope that one day, medicine will advance to the point where the clitoris of an adult can be activated to grow into a full-sized penis – so that transmen could grow their own penis, instead of having to undergo extensive surgery to create a neo phallus.

The sensitivity of the clitoris may also increase, although that might just be because of a heightened libido, not because of any physiological change.

HAIR GROWTH

Testosterone will cause you to sprout more body hair in all the usual male places: chest, belly, buttocks, arms, legs, face, and back. The amount and distribution varies, just as it does with bio men. Personally I have a fur coat on my belly, but not nearly as much hair as I would like on my chest. A fur coat on my chest would be great because it would cover my scars, but it's not going to happen. On the other hand, the hair on my forearms and legs has become much thicker, which is great. I have almost no hair on my back, but I am just fine with that! I know one trans man who was so disgusted by the thick pelt of hair that grew on his back that he had to stop testosterone.

Facial hair growth is an important issue for many transmen, for the obvious reason that it sends a clear message of masculinity to the world. Almost all transmen go through a period when strangers may not be sure of their gender. This is not a fun place to be. But since I grew a soul patch and a beard, no one ever reads me as female.

Hair Loss

While hair on the rest of your body increases, the hair on your head will definitely decrease. Your hair will become thinner, and male pattern baldness will start to set in. This happens to almost all men, whether bio or trans. Many transmen will end up totally bald. The general consensus is that the degree of hair loss is genetic – so look at your father or brothers to see how your hair loss is likely to progress.

Fat, Muscle, and Strength Changes

Taking testosterone will most likely lead to a decrease in your overall body fat, but will redistribute fat from your buttocks and hips towards your stomach. I am always amazed when I see pre-T photos of myself, and realize how comparatively enormous my buttocks used to be. On the other hand, I still carry some fat on my hips, which is disappointing. And one of the first things I noticed after my mastectomy was how enormous my belly suddenly looked! It had always been hidden and dwarfed by my breasts, but after the mastectomy I could clearly notice that I had acquired a classic middle-aged male style belly.

I have always struggled with my weight, and the

testosterone has actually helped me, but it was no magic bullet. However, over time it has definitely made my body appear more wiry and masculine, rather than round and chubby. Of course, I have to work with it – I still put on weight during vacations, and have to work hard to get rid of the excess weight. And I am still a long way from being thin. Also, testosterone has the opposite effect on some transmen, causing increased appetite, weight gain, and fluid retention.

Testosterone has two primary effects: anabolic and androgenic. The androgenic effects are the various effects that make you more masculine. The anabolic effects primarily result in the stimulation of muscle and bone growth, as well as metabolic changes. So your muscles will become stronger and denser. In particular, your upper body strength will increase. Before I started testosterone I could not do a single push-up, but now I can easily do 30 at a time. The change was amazing. This increased strength persists, even though I no longer work out with weights. I now achieve more with a few sets of pushups than I used to achieve with endless hours in the gym.

Changes in the Blood

Testosterone causes major changes in your blood, which is one reason why it is so important to be monitored by medical professionals. Changes include elevated blood lipids (cholesterol and triglycerides) and an increase in the number of red blood cells. On the positive side, this increase may lead to an increased ability to perform athletically. On the negative side, if the number gets too high, you can develop a syndrome called polycythemia, which is potentially dangerous. The main treatment for polycythemia (apart from prevention) is bloodletting.

As mentioned previously, due to lack of medical monitoring I developed polycythemia. However it was not severe enough to warrant blood letting. But since then, I donate blood regularly. This is a great way to keep my red blood cells under control and do a good deed at the same time.

ACNE

Some transmen get acne due to the hormonal changes. I have heard it said that if you had acne during adolescence, you will get it again when you start T. However, I had severe acne for years during adolescence, and I have had no acne at all since I started testosterone.

If you develop acne, you will need to consult with your doctor for solutions. Some men report that the form in which they take their testosterone has an impact. Injectable testosterone comes in a suspension, and it may be the suspension causing the problem. So experiment with different brands of testosterone and different suspensions if you have problems with acne.

THE IMPACT OF SEX REASSIGNMENT SURGERIES ON TESTOSTERONE

Having sex reassignment surgeries such as a mastectomy and a hysterectomy is likely to have a significant impact on the way your testosterone dose impacts your body. Little research has been done. However, we do know the way that testosterone works on the body, and can make logical deductions about the probable impact of the surgeries.

Once testosterone is in your body, it converts to either of two metabolites: estrogen or DHT (a more potent androgen responsible for things like beard growth, genital growth, and male pattern balding). The testosterone that converts to estrogen is converted by an enzyme called aromatase. There are many aromatase receptors in ovarian, breast, and fat tissues. Therefore, it is logical to assume that less of your testosterone will convert to estrogen once you have a mastectomy and a hysterectomy. Certainly there is a lot of anecdotal evidence of masculinization (such as beard growth, muscle growth, and head-hair loss) speeding up after these surgeries.

The hope is that after these surgeries you will need a lower dose of testosterone to maintain the same testosterone levels. However, I cannot say that happened in my case. I had my surgeries years ago, and have not been able to decrease my testosterone dosage.

POSSIBLE NEGATIVE EFFECTS OF TESTOSTERONE

Some people experience mood swings and increased aggression, but this appears to be unusual. I have not experienced this personally at all. However, I notice that my anger has a different quality – it is much more sudden and aggressive, but burns out very quickly. In other words, I have flashes of intense anger that I have not experienced before, but they dissipate quickly and do no harm (apart from the fact that my sudden yelling sometimes frightens the dogs). It seems to me that in certain circumstances of primitive life these flashes of energizing fury could have been life saving, so perhaps it is an evolutionary aspect of testosterone.

Another effect that may be perceived as negative is loss of hair on the top of your head – male pattern balding. Bio men sometimes use DHT blocking drugs such as Finestride to prevent balding. However, as balding is part of the package deal, so to speak, of masculinization, it would seem to make little sense for a trans man to take DHT blocking drugs (after all, we want most of the changes, such as beard growth and genital growth).

Some transmen don't have a problem with balding. Certainly, classic male pattern balding (receding hair on two sides of your head) goes a long way towards presenting as male. It definitely helped me enormously. I have even heard of transmen who have plucked their hair or shaved parts of their head to simulate male pattern balding in the early days of transition. I also know many men who have gone completely bald and grown beards, thus essentially moving their hair about ten inches south. This of course creates a completely male appearance that guarantees you will never again be called "Ma'am."

If the idea of complete baldness really worries you, you might consider trying Rogaine. My endocrinologist assured me it works, so I have been on it for years. I have lost some hair, but certainly not all of it. I find it works better if I follow the directions and use it twice a day. This has the negative side effect that it stains my pillowcase yellow, but that's better than not having any hair! Be warned that it definitely will stain your pillowcase if you use it before bedtime. It even stains the pillow underneath the pillow case. But replacing a pillow and pillow case is a lot cheaper than hair implants, after all.

CHAPTER 3: PASSING AS A MAN

Once I began my transition, I became obsessed with passing as a man. This became more intense as I became more masculinized. People were increasingly confused about my gender, and life became very uncomfortable. I could not go out for long because I was afraid to use both the female *and* the male washrooms. Fortunately we had one non-gendered washroom at work. However, I started to work very hard on passing as a man, anxious to get out of the gender twilight zone and blend in like an average man.

HAIR STYLE

Your hairstyle has an enormous impact on passing as a man. I had difficulty getting a masculine haircut. Hairdressers tended to want to feminize me – subconsciously, perhaps. And I felt embarrassed to just out and out say that I wanted a male haircut. Once I went to a barbershop, and they turned me away, saying that they only cut men's hair. This was intensely embarrassing. I had hoped to pass, but failed.

The solution I found was a gay man who was trans friendly, who cut hair out of his own home. I explained my situation and he gave me an appropriate haircut. This catapulted me forward in my quest to appear more masculine.

Nowadays I have a barbershop that I go to, and no one ever questions my gender there. I even had a beard trim there the other day! And once, just for fun, I went back to the barber shop that turned me away years ago. They cut my hair quite happily. Obviously, I had come a long way in my masculinization process between those two visits.

In any event, try to find someone who will cut your hair appropriately. If you still appear more female than male, this may be difficult. Or you may just be more assertive than me, and take along a picture of a man and insist on getting a haircut like his.

CLOTHING

Clothing is the other major factor in passing. You may already be dressing in masculine clothes before you start your transition. Women can get away with this far more than men. In my case, I bought all my clothes at men's clothing stores. When I still had breasts that was quite stressful, but the staff either didn't notice, or pretended not to.

However, I did not dress one hundred percent masculine before my transition. For example, I did not wear a tie or a men's dress suit. That would have seemed odd to my colleagues (or just odder, perhaps). Only since I pass as a man have I felt comfortable wearing a tie. A tie is a great thing, because it is much like a beard – it is a loud and clear signal that you are a man. When I first started wearing ties, I used Hudson's online resources for transmen to show me how to do it up. I highly recommend that resource. Just Google "Hudson how to tie a tie."

HEIGHT

Sadly, many transmen are short for men, and this makes it that much harder to pass. Testosterone will not change this (unless you start on it when you are still growing, which hardly ever happens). I spent years wearing elevator shoes that I bought online. Eventually I stopped, because my wife told me they looked funny, and they did not make that much difference.

I have now accepted that it is all right to be a very short man. If people are surprised, they take care not to show it. I think it is a social taboo to comment on a man's shortness. My height does not seem to impede my ability to pass. Even though my wife is about three inches taller than me. And my daughters are taller than me, too.

It helps to remember that heights vary amongst bio men as well. I often encounter men who are shorter than me (admittedly, this mainly happens in Mexico). However, the point is that being too short should not stop you from transition, as it will not preclude success. I put off my transition for longer than I should have, and one of the reasons was my height. I thought I could not possibly pass, but I was wrong!

MAN-NERISMS (HOW TO ACT MANLY)

Here's a tip: subscribe to a magazine called *Men's Health*. It's cheap enough if you subscribe, and it will give you tons of advice on how to behave like a man and how to dress like a (well-dressed) man. Not to mention that you will have a very manly moment when your mail arrives and there's a copy of *Men's Health* addressed to Mr. Your Name. The magazine is stuffed full of advice on acting manly, and also has this extra feature in some editions: if you turn it backwards, it becomes a magazine called *Men's Style*. This is full of tips about how to dress, including advice about a lot of very affordable clothes (and some horrendously expensive clothes too). You can also subscribe to this magazine online.

For example, I learned from *Men's Health* that during the next winter, men's fashion would focus on the colors blue and green. This was great, as I love blue, but I had not been sure if it was manly enough, now that I was being accepted everywhere as a mature man. After reading this I knew that I could replace my grey sweater with a bright blue sweater, and not only still be manly, but also subtly convey that I was on the cutting edge of fashion, not some out-of-date old man.

The existence of magazines such as *Men's Health* shows that even bio men need advice on how to be manly. And they were born in male bodies and treated like boys or men their whole lives. They spent hundreds of hours watching other boys being manly. Most of them had fathers who spent endless hours modeling manliness, teaching them how to shave, and just generally trying desperately to ensure their sons were manly.

I've seen it with my two-month-old nephew. Everyone coos over him, calling him "a little bruiser" and saying things like "how's our little man?" It's a little sickening, given that he weighs all of twelve pounds (I weigh more than thirteen times that much, and no one ever calls me a bruiser!). I recall that with my niece, no one ever called her "a little bruiser" (even though she was), or said, "How's our little woman?" She wasn't a "little woman", she was a "little princess" or "a little sweetheart." If she's lucky, she'll get to be called a "woman" by the time she's 21. But bio boys are called men from the day they are born.

Despite all this programming and education, millions of bio men still need advice on how to be manly. So I think it's realistic to assume that most transmen could use some help too. For example, in my early days of transition I kept saying non-manly things like "What do you think?" and "This is just my personal opinion, but ..." and "I don't know how I want my sideburns, what do you think?"

Eventually I started to notice that when I responded to my barber's questions with another question, or (horror of horrors) an apology, he recoiled slightly as if I smelled funny. I soon learned that even if I did not know the answer, I should just say something with absolute authority, as in this dialogue:

Barber: "How do you want your hair?"
Me: "Short." (**Not:** "I'm not sure, what do you think would suit me?")
Barber: "How do you want your sideburns?"
Me: "Straight." (Even though I was secretly thinking, "But I don't have sideburns.")

It was a relief to pick up a copy of *Men's Health* and learn that bio men also have to learn how to be manly. For example, I read an article called "What it Means to be a Man" by Joel Stein. The author confessed that when he learned he was going to have a son, he went into a panic because he thought he was not manly enough to be a role model for his son. He had always been the geek type, and had avoided all the traditionally male activities, like camping, sports, fishing, football, and plumbing. So in preparation for being the father of a son, he manically threw himself into all kinds of manly stuff, and made this interesting discovery:

"What you actually do determines who you are. Just as smiling actually makes you happy, doing manly things makes you manly. And manliness is self-perpetuating, because every time you push yourself to try something difficult, you become less afraid of everything else. ... The lesson that behavior trumps personality would be obvious if not for our Freudian culture, which teaches us that we are black boxes and that if we rummage deeply enough in the darkness we can find our souls. But ... to actually change, you have to go out and do stuff. We're not black boxes. We're the sum of our experiences."

Stein actually wrote a whole book about this quest, called *Man Made: A Stupid Quest for Masculinity* (available on Amazon and a good, funny read). In any event, *Men's Health* will give you some good advice on how to act like a man, so as to pass as a man and be accepted as a man.

Apart from that, we are surrounded by bio men, so just watch, learn, and copy. It is very easy to observe and learn, and slowly start to modify your behaviors. Moreover, it is quite a circular process. The more you look and act like a man, the more people will treat you like a man, which will cause you to act more like a man.

As an example, people will expect you to be able to do all kinds of things once you transition, such as fix things, and carry things. You will be stronger, but if you were already not very technical, you will not magically become technical. However, you can certainly take the trouble to learn more than the average girl is taught. You may find yourself doing some unexpectedly very manly things around the office or home. This will make people treat you more like a man, which will make you feel more manly.

Early in my transition I went to buy a used bicycle from a man. The saddle was too high, and needed to be adjusted before I could try the bike out. The seller simply handed me a tool to do it. I realized that in my entire life up to that point, in that situation the other man would have done it for me. I was really flustered, as I had never actually done that for myself before. Since then I have taken some lessons and done some reading, and I actually quite enjoy working on my bike. I also enjoy that I can lift it around very easily, as I am now much stronger. The strength was a side effect of the testosterone; I had to work on the bike knowledge.

Somewhere in all this you will need to decide what kind of man you want to be, and this is a big bonus. For example, I choose not be Homer Simpson. Or George Bush. Or Stephen Harper. But I'm not saintly enough to pull off Gandhi. So I am still looking for my perfect father figure (even though I am now a grandfather). But I know he's out there somewhere. I have a lot of times when I want to be Bruce Willis, but I know I will never be quite manly enough to pull that off. However, I have taken a leaf or two from Schwarzenegger (I lift weights and I never run). But of course I am ignoring his choice in motor vehicles.

VOICE

Most transmen will never have voices that are as deep as those of bio men. However, your voice will definitely get lower. Mine is far from as low as I would like it to be. However, I can drop it down a few octaves if I consciously try. Of course, it's impossible to remember to do this all the time.

It is possible to get professional voice training, but this is expensive. Personally I don't find it necessary. There are bio men out there with relatively high voices. My voice does not prevent me from passing as a man.

FACIAL HAIR

Growing some facial hair is one of the fastest ways to pass as a man. Unfortunately, it takes time for testosterone to cause your facial hair to grown. And some transmen never have enough facial hair to grow a reasonable moustache or beard. At the moment I have a small goatee and soul patch, but I have never been able to grow sideburns.

Facial hair growth varies a lot, with some transmen

being able to grow impressive beards, and others having a lot less. I can grow a soul patch and modest beard, but my sideburns will not grow. However, two things are certain: you will definitely have some facial hair growth, and you will definitely have to start shaving.

Some people think that shaving stimulates facial hair growth, but there is no proof of that. It has never helped me. Some transmen use Rogaine to stimulate facial hair growth, but this is not medically recommended.

Even if you only have peach fuzz on your face, I highly recommend that you start shaving. It is better to have no facial hair than to have soft fuzz. Only boys and women have soft peach fuzz. Adult men have smoothly shaven faces or stubble. So if you want to be read as male, you need to shave, even before you have much facial hair.

BREASTS

Nothing says "female" quite as clearly as a pair of breasts. If you have very large breasts, it makes passing as a man very difficult.

Some transmen have top surgery to achieve a male-looking chest. However, not every transman can afford or access this surgery. Also, most of us have to wait years to have it. Therefore, many of us spend a lot of time living with breasts that prevent us from passing as men, or make it very difficult. If you have really small breasts you can hide them with baggy shirts, but many men who have large breasts have to resort to binding.

There are resources on the Internet that will help you with binding. I am not going to write about it because I have no personal experience of it, and because it can be dangerous if done too tightly. I am not saying don't do it, because I have no right to say that. I completely understand why some transmen bind their breasts. I used to have very large breasts, and once I started transitioning, these caused me great embarrassment. They also made it very hard for me to pass. The only reason I did not bind is that I was afraid of doing it, as it has been known to cause injury. Also, I worked out a lot, and I needed to be able to breathe freely.

Somehow, I managed to pass with those large breasts, eventually. I will never be sure how that happened. But I am not the only transman who has had that experience. It seems that people see what they want to see, or what they expect to see.

Of course, if you can access surgery to remove your breasts, your ability to pass as a man will catapult forward. The relief I felt after my breast removal surgery was overwhelming. It's been years now, and I am still frequently feel overcome with gratitude that I now have a male-looking chest. It is no doubt the second-biggest factor in my passing as a man (the first is being on T).

PACKING

Whether or not to pack is an issue every transman has to decide for himself. In talking to transmen over the years, I have heard some very different opinions on the matter. While I think it's true that most people don't look hard at other people's crotches, there are situations in which the lack of a bulge could be a major giveaway. For example, men in cycling pants have very obvious bulges. A man who lacked this bulge would stand out – or fail to stand out! Similarly the lack of a bulge could be very obvious in swimming trunks, unless they are very baggy. And personally I think it's very obvious when people wear wet suits, as well. It can also be fairly obvious in tighter dress pants and jeans, as well as sweat pants.

On the other hand, I have come across transmen who have never packed, and who insist that it does not detract from their ability to pass as men. According to them, no one has ever noticed their lack of a crotch bulge.

PACKERS THAT DEPRESS

Also, some men choose not to pack for psychological reasons. For example, I remember one man who said that putting a packer in his pants every morning would only serve to remind him, every morning, that he did not have a penis ... and that would depress him. So he did not pack at all, and said that no one had ever noticed.

PACKERS THAT MAKE A MAN FEEL COMPLETE

Several men say that they don't feel complete without their packers. Many transmen agree they would not be seen in public without their packers – it makes them feel more complete, and makes them feel more secure about passing. I tend to agree with that. Certainly when I am out cycling with friends, I feel they would notice if I was not packing. After all, every other male cyclist has a conspicuous crotch bulge, so why wouldn't I have one?

One man said that the weight of his Mr. Right packer gives him a solid reminder of who he is. I've got one of those, and on days when I wear it, I have to agree with him. It's got a wonderfully heavy, solid feeling. It makes me feel more solidly centered in my masculinity when I wear it. However, it is kind of heavy for everyday wear.

My favorite packer is made by Reel Magik. This company sells a variety of prosthetics, and has an FTM Prosthesis Store. They do extremely realistic but extremely expensive prosthetic penises, which can be made to order to match your hair and skin color. However, they also offer what they call their basic packer, which is under a hundred dollars, but pleasingly realistic as they use the same mold that they use for their medical prosthetic. It has 3-D testicles, and is in my opinion the most realistic and pleasing packer you can get for less than a hundred dollars. It straddles the line between packer and prosthetic. It also does not have to be powdered; the only maintenance it requires is an occasional wash.

PACKING WHILE SWIMMING

Now that I've had my top surgery and I can swim in just male trunks, I always pack while swimming. I think it's useful for passing. The other day I was in a public swimming pool and I overheard a group of women discussing some poor man. One woman said, "He was in a Speedo, and there was nothing there!" That reminded me that some women *are* looking, and you will be noticed if you are not packing while swimming. That's not going to happen to me.

So in order to pass, I always wear a packer when swimming. Of course you have to be sure that you don't drop your packer while swimming. I find I can dive and swim vigorously with my packer simply tucked into my Speedo. However, I usually prefer to be safer than that. What I have done is purchase a swim bikini from an online seller, Mensuas. It has an adjustable and detachable ring built in to hold your packer. The ring is great – it has Velcro on it, which you tie around the top of your packer. Once you have that in place, your packer is secure, no matter what you do in the water. For this reason it is also useful for other times when you are packing. However, the point about this bikini is that it is designed to go in the water, so it stands up to water pretty well, dries quickly, and of course, holds your packer safely. As I don't quite have the body to pull off wearing just a bikini, I always wear swim trunks over top. But I do have the peace of mind of knowing that when my swim trunks get wet and cling to me, no one is going to look at me and wonder what's wrong with me.

Underwear for Packing

You also need to think about keeping your packer in place when wearing regular clothes. I have heard of men who have actually had their packer fall out of their pants, and somehow survived that experience. However, I would find that extremely embarrassing. Consequently, I have spent many hours of my life fussing about what kind of underwear to wear to keep my packer firmly in place.

I finally solved the problem with an online supplier of underwear designed specifically for FTMs – TranZwear (http://www.tranzwear.net/). This company is run by a transman and customizes products to order. For example, you could get yourself seven pairs of Dockers boxer briefs, with sewn-in rings to hold your packers, and (if you wanted) sewn-in cloth loops (called cages) to hold your packer's balls in place. You can choose which extras you want with your underwear. I have tried them all, and highly recommend that you try the type that have ring plus cage, as these really do a great job of holding your packer in the right place. Since I got these, I have never had to worry again. And believe me, it can be a worry. It might seem acceptable to just put your packer in regular underwear – but sooner or later you may forget, and your packer could, for example, come tumbling out onto a dirty washroom floor. Tranzwear offers very affordable peace of mind.

CHAPTER 4:
COMING OUT AS TRANSGENDERED

COMING OUT AS TRANSGENDERED
TO FRIENDS AND FAMILY

All aspects of transitioning are challenging, but coming out is often the most challenging of all. By coming out, I mean telling your family and friends that you plan to transition your outward gender presentation. I am not referring to disclosing to the world that you have not always lived as a man. This is another kind of coming out (see below, under the heading, "Should You be Stealth?").

You may have felt like a man inside for years, but very often, people who know you will not have realized that. They may be profoundly shocked when you tell them. Something that seems logical and desirable to you may seem anything but for other people when you tell them. Usually, the most difficult people to talk to are your closest family members. They usually have the most invested in you, and the most fixed ideas of who you are. In addition, your transition may directly impact their sense of their own identity. Parents in particular seem to find it very hard to accept transitioning gender.

Of course, there have been some heartwarming stories recently of parents accepting and affirming their child's transition choice.

On the other hand, there was the sad story of Leelah Alcorn, a teenager who stepped in front of a moving tractor-trailer truck in December of 2014 in Union Township, Pennsylvania. In her blog, Leelah blamed her Christian parents for refusing to accept that she was female. After her death, her parent's continued to refer to Leelah as "he," and blamed the truck driver. Leelah is just one of many such teenagers – she just happens to be one that we know about.

Suicide rates among transgendered youth are high, and escalate when the youth don't have parental support. Suicide rates remain higher among gender-nonconforming people for our entire lives (Haas et al.). It can be a tough way to live, and people can be very non-accepting.

Even before you come out, you will probably have some idea of how your family is likely to react. If you are certain it will be a negative reaction, you would be well advised to get some support structures in place first. There are even cases where coming out can put you in physical danger – such as being beaten or evicted. If you think this is likely to happen, make sure you take whatever precautions you can.

In my case I did not anticipate any violent reactions, but I still made sure that the first person I told was a trusted friend who I knew would be supportive. She was, and remains so to this day. I very much appreciate her years of unconditional support and love.

But of course it is easier for friends, because their identities are not as much invested in our definition of who we are. For spouses, parents, siblings, and children, the change is profound. A daughter becomes a son; a wife becomes a husband; a sister becomes a brother; a mom becomes a dad. These are big changes in anybody's book. Many people experience it as the loss of a daughter, wife, sister, or mother. This has to be very traumatic.

However, at the end of the day, the people around us have to accept us, or we have to move on without them. Most of us do not feel we have any choice but to be who we are, and if everybody doesn't love this, there is not a lot we can do about it. We can give people books about the subject, we can try to explain and educate. But fundamentally we cannot change other people very much. We just have to do our best to be ourselves, and hope that others can cope and be respectful.

COMING OUT TO MY MOTHER

My own father is long dead, so he does not know about my transition. My mother still has a lot trouble with it, even though it has been many years since I told her. She loves me and wants me to be happy, so she does not openly oppose it. But I can tell that at root she does not understand, and thinks it is all just some kind of game I am playing. She still forgets pronouns almost every time she talks about me, referring to me as "she." She almost chokes on "he." Fortunately most of her friends are half-deaf, and don't seem to notice. Moreover, people hear what they expect to hear. I have had a couple of talks with her about it, and she is mildly apologetic, but she does not change.

I have spoken with many transmen in this situation, and it seems to be quite common. It could be worse, and I am done worrying about it. It does however mean that there are certain social situations I have to exclude her from. As I am stealth about my trans status, I don't want to risk having her call me "she" in front of people who have only ever known me as male.

COMING OUT TO MY SIBLINGS

I have no idea how my brother feels about my transition, as he has never discussed it, and did not reply to the email I sent to tell him about it. However, he is quite conservative, so I am pretty sure he is both baffled and disapproving. It is unfortunate, because his kids are very young, and I would have liked them to grow up thinking of me as their uncle, not their aunt. It's just creating potential confusion and discomfort down the road. I am pretty sure he and his wife refer to me as female, yet their children see that I look 100% male. It is probably fortunate that they live so far away that I hardly ever see them.

My sister is supportive, and responded to my disclosure email with a supportive email. By the way, I am not specifically recommending coming out to people via email – my sister and my brother live thousands of miles away, which is why I came out to them by email. On the other hand, an email does give you the chance to calmly and rationally explain what you are doing, so in some situations it is probably a good choice.

Of course, if the reaction is likely to be violent, it is also a safe choice, as you don't have to be in the same room.

Coming Out to My Wife

My wife was initially resistant. She said she had not signed up for a husband when she married me (we are fortunate enough to live in a place where same-sex marriage is legal, so we were legally married before my transition). We had some tough conversations and difficult times. But she did come around after a while. As she says, I am still the same person, only happier.

My wife is my strongest supporter now. I don't know how I would have got through my surgeries and my recoveries without her. She was an absolute rock of uncomplaining support throughout them. And I am not the easiest patient, as I tend to be very anxious, and I recover slowly.

My wife makes a point of introducing me very clearly as her husband. We are still not the most mainstream couple, given that I am three inches shorter than her and have smaller hands and feet! As I have said to her, we are still a queer couple, just queer in a different way. I should not make light of it, because I know it was a major identity shift for her. She identified as straight for years, then met me and changed her identity to lesbian. She came out to everyone as a lesbian – and a few years later, she kind of had to take that back. That would be challenging for anyone. But she has come through it like a superstar.

Coming Out to My Children

My children were tricky. I have three children, none of them my biological children, but I have parented all three of them since birth, so to me (and I am sure to them) they are as much my children as if they were my biological offspring. They were all pretty young when I started transitioning, and just got used to me being more and more masculine over the years. But then I got to the stage that I was going to publicly and officially transition – name change; legal gender change; passport change. I was also at the point where I was no longer prepared to be referred to as "she." I just got to a point where I could not do it any more, not for one more day.

Of course it had been building for a while (over fifty years!) At that point, I *had* to tell them. I told each one individually, and they each took it differently. Bear in mind that I have an ex-commonlaw wife who is their mother, so they still had a mom – they just didn't have two moms any more. I told them they could call me by my first name if they felt odd calling me "Dad." I said "Mom" was no longer going to be appropriate. To get their buy-in on this, I pointed out that people would think they were crazy if they were calling a man "Mom." All three of them have gone with calling me by my first name, with very few slips to "Mom." It seems that kids' minds are more flexible than senior minds.

The youngest had nothing to say, and I still don't know how she feels. She doesn't seem to have a problem with it, though. The middle one was quite upset, and said that no matter what happens, I will always be her mother. Five years on, and she now introduces me as her father, but still does not call me "Dad." However, she also doesn't call me "Mom." The oldest one is most supportive, and always refers to me as her dad. She has asked me what I want from her, and said that she just wants me to be happy, and will support me in whatever way I request. I know that when she is at my ex-wife's home, she corrects the family at the dinner table if they refer to me as "she." As they are a very politically correct family, I think she shames them a bit.

COMING OUT TO MY STEP-CHILDREN

Then there are my step-kids. I came out to them via email, because I don't have the closest of relationships with them. Step-kids are tricky, especially if you meet them when they are already adults. Then of course they are really not step-kids at all, except legally. They are the children of my wife, and therefore part of my family. But they are obviously not my children – they are not children at all! I am not sure how they think about it.

My stepson consistently seems to forget about it completely, and when he remembers, I think he finds it really difficult to deal with. But at least he treats me politely and respectfully. His wife tries harder to be supportive, and uses male pronouns.

They have very young kids, and we have fixed on a gender-neutral name for me. They already had a granddad. I hope they grow up thinking of me as male. I know they mainly do, but I also know the five-year-old recently asked my wife if I was a boy or a girl. So I suspect she is getting contradictory messages at home, as my presentation is unequivocally male. Oh well; no one said life during or after transition would be simple and uncomplicated. All in all, I have it pretty good. Many people have to leave their families and start new lives. I have been able to retain all of my family and most of my friends.

In terms of friends, no one has openly broken with me, but I notice that I see less of some of the people I used to know, notably lesbians who were just casual friends. I feel no loss. As is no doubt apparent, I have more than enough people in my life.

COMING OUT AT WORK

Coming out at work was incredibly tough and stressful. The company I worked for was quite conservative, but no doubt afraid of lawsuits, so they did a kind of minimal acceptance. I was never persecuted, but I was also never supported in any way. By sheer luck the building had one gender-neutral washroom (as there was only one washroom for people with disabilities, they had to designate it gender-neutral). If it wasn't for that, I would have had to quit, because they weren't going to make any special accommodations for me, and going to the men's washroom would have been horribly awkward. I know some people would have the courage to do that, but I did not. I knew that all of those men still perceived me as female (and at that stage, I had not even had my top surgery, and was 100% biologically female). I just could not see suddenly showing up in their washroom. Sometimes I feel like that was cowardly of me. But my wife has reminded me that I was in an extremely vulnerable place at that time in my life.

I eventually solved the problem by getting a new job. In that job, everyone has known me as male from day one, and there is no problem at all. Not from my colleagues, anyway. But I still went through the stresses that many people who transition go through. For the first year I worried about being "found out." I had not moved cities, and I knew that at any time, my past life could be revealed to one of my colleagues. It's been two and a half years now, and all seems fine.

For the first year, I also had nightmares about washroom situations. I would dream that I was somehow exposed as female in the men's room. I ended up seeing a counselor about that for a while. Now I am completely over that. I still feel sad and somewhat anxious about the fact that I cannot pee standing up. I worry that other men will notice that I am always in the stall, not at the urinal. But there is nothing I can do about that one. I have been approved for surgeries that would give me that ability, but at my age (and given the fact that I don't come through surgeries well), I am not going to risk it. My plumbing works perfectly well for its two most important purposes (elimination and pleasure), and I am not willing to risk losing that. There are stand-to-pee devices one can buy (see the final chapter on "Online Resources") – but I have never really been able to get those to work for me. At the end of the day, I don't think other men really notice or care what I do in the washroom. I know I don't notice or care what they do!

COMING OUT TO EVERYBODY ELSE

Until I transitioned, I did not realize how many people are involved in my life. I discovered that I also had to come out to doctors, dentists, medical specialists, physiotherapists, massage therapists, counselors … you name it. It was exhausting! More importantly, I found that it posed an important question for me: should I come out to them, or just create a whole new world of support professionals?

The problem with staying with the same professionals is that they all know you as female, and most of them will have difficulty in shifting their mindset. To this day, I cannot tell you what a relief it is when I meet someone (such as a new dentist) who has never known me as anything but a man. Obviously, they never make mistakes with pronouns, and they don't treat me as anything but just an average man. I really love that, and find it so relaxing – and validating.

By contrast, let's take the example of the dental practice where I had been going for about twenty years. They were a politically correct office, so they dutifully changed their records and started sending me reminders addressed to "Mr." However, the dentist, the assistants, and the hygienists would keep forgetting and calling me "she." I found the usual misery of going to the dentist compounded by the fresh misery of being unable to speak while a crew of people around me bounced from "he" to "she" and back to "he."

Then there was the visit to my cardiologist. He had not seen me for about three years, and suddenly, there I was again – no longer presenting as female, but now as a transitioning man. I could almost feel the disapproval coming off him in waves, although of course he gritted his teeth and got through it professionally. To compound matters, he had an intern with him, so both of them got to disapprove of me together. I felt incredibly disempowered. While I was going through the experience, I was too overwhelmed to walk away from it. In any event, I could not have walked away from it even if I had the strength to do it, because I was seeing him to get a medical clearance for top surgery. I found myself in the disempowered situation of desperately needing someone who clearly disapproved of me. He cleared me for the surgery, and afterwards I told my doctor that if I ever needed a cardiologist again, I would like her to find me a new one.

The doctor's office was another nightmare. The doctor was great and very supportive. However, her staff kept forgetting that I had transitioned. A full year after I had transitioned, one of them phoned me to remind me to come in for a pap smear! I was at work when I got that call, and I actually had a couple of nightmares after that about what would have happened if my phone had been on speaker when I took that phone call!

In retrospect, if I were doing it all over again, I would have changed as many of these support people in my life as possible when I transitioned. Transitioning is a tremendous journey. It takes unshakable faith in yourself, and a firm belief that you can do it. To have a whole host of people constantly undermining this faith and belief is very tough. On the other hand, surrounding yourself with as many people as possible who see you as nothing but male helps you in your own mental transition. It took me a long time to feel confident in my new social role as male, and every person who called me "Sir" helped me a bit. Every person who called me "she" dragged me back a little.

You may think that you are totally clear in your male identity, and that it won't matter how other people treat you. And you may be right, and I hope you are. But for me personally, despite having been so male-identified my entire life, it took me a long time to move into my new social-gender role and feel safe and confident there. I needed every bit of support I could find, and I really did not need the unintentional undermining of casually thoughtless other people.

On the other hand, I kept the same counselor who had acted as a marriage counselor for my wife and me. I was worried about her reaction, and immensely relieved when her response was: "Well, it's about time!" That was immensely validating. She has also been very affirming in the months since then, with many compliments on what a positive change I have made in my life, and how successfully I have made it. So I would not change her for the world!

SHOULD YOU BE STEALTH?

This is such a tough one. There are pros and cons to coming out as trans, just as there are pros and cons about being stealth. At the end of the day, it will come down to what you are most comfortable with.

I know people who live rich and fulfilling lives being out – and also people who live rich and fulfilling lives being stealth. For myself, it was not even a question. I always knew I was going to be stealth. In fact, a large part of my motivation to finally transition completely was that I was tired of feeling like a gender anomaly. I needed to blend in and live my life without people always looking at me.

Nowadays I mainly have that. Just occasionally in public places I will become aware of someone staring at me. My small size is probably the reason. I kind of look like a miniature man. However, a stranger would not know whether I was transgendered, or had some kind of growth disorder, or just had the bad luck to have two incredibly short parents! I am not odd enough looking to provoke people to attack me – just odd enough for someone on a bus, with nothing better to do, to notice, get puzzled, and stare for a minute. Then I look back, they look away, and life goes on. It is a whole lot better than it used to be. I don't have men screaming insults at me from their truck windows, for example. I don't fear being attacked. Most of the time I just blend in, like just any other boring, middle-aged man. I love that!

Chapter 5: All About Hair

Since I went on testosterone I have grown hair pretty much all over my body. I have a nice pelt across my stomach, and I have hair in every nook and cranny of my privates. I even have a little hair growing on my back now. And since my mastectomy, I am finally starting to grow some hair on my chest. It will be a long time before it covers my scars, though – probably never.

All this hair does brings up fresh problems though – namely, how to cope with it all. Especially hair in the nose, which is not attractive, and also very ticklish. I discovered that for about thirty dollars one can buy a nose hair trimmer, which is effective and is a very worthwhile investment.

Treatment for Hair Loss

After seven years on T, I still had no sign of any sideburns. I could grow a pretty good moustache, soul patch, and goatee, but my sideburns just weren't happening. Which really depressed me, because I think sideburn stubble is very masculine, and I really wanted to have some. At the same time, the testosterone was having an effect on my head hair – causing it to basically move from my head to my comb.

So I decided to kill two birds with one stone, and get some Rogaine to work on my hair and my sideburns.

Does Rogaine Work?

My endocrinologist told me Rogaine works, which is why I decided to try it. Everyone agrees that you should allow two to four months before you can expect to see any results from Rogaine, and you should use it faithfully twice a day, every day. Which I did. I was pretty surprised to notice that the hair loss from my head seemed to slow down almost immediately. And it has stayed slowed down. Over the course of a decade my hair has become noticeably thinner, but at least I do still have hair.

I knew not to expect overnight results, so I was patient. And I followed instructions. Applying Rogaine every single morning and every single evening without fail to the recommended parts of the hair on my head, and also to the place where my non-existent sideburns should have been. I also applied some to my arms and the back of my hands. Of course, it is not medically recommended to apply Rogaine to the face, arms, or hands. It might have done me some harm, for all I know. So I am definitely *not* recommending it to anyone.

At about five weeks, I started to see blond hairs growing on my cheeks where my sideburns should be. This was very encouraging. If I looked hard, in bright sunlight, I could even see one of two dark wispy hairs where my sideburns should be. Unfortunately, most of those were growing out of my solitary mole. Still, at the time I thought it was a start. Now I know that it wasn't, and I am reconciled to the fact that I will never have sideburns.

This makes me reflect that there is nothing quite like adolescence at middle age to make one self-centered. I am sure no teenage boy has ever studied his nascent whiskers as hard as I have studied mine. Slightly pathetic, really, given that no one else ever seems to notice anything at all ... it's all just too sparse and blond.

After more than a year on Rogaine, the results for me were as follows: my sideburns were still pathetic, and I gave up putting the Rogaine on my cheeks. However, I have thicker hair on my arms and more hair on my hands, so that worked, and definitely helps to make me look more masculine. I even have hair on my upper arms, and I think that is entirely from the Rogaine. My hair loss on my head has slowed down, and I am very happy about that. So in sum, it seems that Rogaine works to stimulate hair growth, but only in places where you are genetically predisposed to grow it. It also works better when it is used exactly as recommended on the label.

Is Rogaine Safe for Transmen?

Rogaine is packaged with a warning that it is not to be used by women. This is a bit confusing for transmen. However, I just ignored it. The truth is that Rogaine is now marketing pretty much exactly the same product for women, so they must have tested it on women as well. So wherever you are on your transition journey, you should be fine. Of course, I am not a doctor – this is just my layman opinion.

Make Sure you Get Rogaine Foam!

Luckily I read about this before I ordered four month's worth. Rogaine Original is oily and messy, from all accounts. Rogaine Foam is foamy and not messy. So if you decide to try Rogaine, make sure you order Rogaine Foam (unless you actually *want* an oily head for some reason).

Application Tip for Rogaine

The instructions say to run your hands under cold water before applying so that the foam does not melt too fast. Yes, you should do that. But rather than following their instructions to put the Rogaine you are going to use onto the palm of your hand, try squirting it onto the basin. That way it will melt even slower, giving you more time to apply it correctly. Or just spray it directly onto your head. Experiment and see what works for you.

Bear in mind that it is messy stuff, and that applying it at night will result in yellow stains to your bed linen and pillow.

Order your Rogaine from the United States

If you live in Canada and try to order Rogaine 5%, you will be out of luck – it's illegal without a prescription in Canada. You could try to get a prescription from your doctor or endocrinologist – or you could just order some from the States. It arrives in an inconspicuous package, and I have never yet had it intercepted at the border.

Alternatively I have seen it for sale in Shoppers Drug Mart in Canada, but it is only a 2% solution. Based on my own experience, I would be very surprised if that worked.

SHAVING

As transmen we usually don't have the opportunity to learn how to shave from our fathers, which is a pity. However, there are many online guides, and it's really not too hard. The most important thing I learned is to buy a decent razor. A pink plastic thing intended for your girlfriend's legs is just not going to cut it. I use a battery-powered Gillette, and one day I may progress to an electric razor (although my barber advises against it, saying that it pulls the hairs out before cutting them, so the hairs are actually cut below the skin, which can lead to rashes).

I do find that the quality of my shaving experience is directly linked to the amount of money I spend on the razor. With a good razor you have a more pleasant shave, and are less likely to cut yourself.

DESIGNER STUBBLE

Designer stubble is a very cool look, commonly seen on many celebrity men. It's also a very rugged and masculine look, and as such very desirable for transmen who are anxious to pass as men. However, it cannot be achieved merely by neglecting to shave for a few days – this will just make you look lazy and messy. I used to think that that cool five o'clock shadow look was just an accident: now I know that men spend a lot of time achieving that look!

The trick to designer stubble includes having a plan, and having a really good razor with adjustable lengths. You need something that allows you to adjust the length of the shave by simply turning a lock wheel. You then need to grow out all your facial hair for at least a week. Many of us transmen have less vigorous facial hair growth, so it might be more like two weeks. Once you have a decent amount of hair to work with, you are ready to go.

Basically what you do is trim all the hair on a number 3 or number 2 setting, then tidy up your jawline, your soul patch, your cheeks, your mustache, and your sideburns with a razor. You want to end up with clean lines that look precise and planned – not a random mess of hair. A nice clean border of hair along your jawline can create a much more angular, masculine look, giving your face more definition.

For further information on this, Google AlphaMconsulting Beard Grooming for Men Designer Stubble. You will find a great video in which professional male image consultant Aaron Marino shows you how to grow, trim, and maintain the perfect designer stubble. He does the video with amusing style – well worth a watch. I found him very instructive, and finally achieved a look that was halfway decent by following his advice. Unfortunately, I don't have dark hair, so the look is less impressive. Still, as he says, no one has perfect facial hair. It's reassuring to hear that bio men struggle with this too!

CHAPTER 6: TIPS FOR SURGERY

The successful outcome of any surgeries you have will depend on many factors that are outside your control. However, what you can do is prepare thoroughly, and be ready with everything you need for a good recovery. Here are a number of tips, based on my own experiences.

- Have some CDs or books lined up to try to stave off depression from the forced inactivity.
- Lay in several weeks worth of groceries so you won't have to go shopping, because that is way too strenuous.
- Your groceries should include lots of high quality health food, as your body needs this to heal itself and recover back to full strength.
- I highly recommend Vitamin C and a multivitamin. The benefits of Vitamin C for healing are fairly well proven, and the multivitamin could be useful if your appetite is down for a while (mine always is after surgery).
- I believe in the benefits of taking Traumeel, a naturopathic remedy that is said to help the body heal. However, there is no scientific proof that it really works.
- Start taking stool softeners the day before surgery, and take them for a few days afterwards until you have your first bowel movement. After that, you can stop the stool softeners, but do continue to eat plenty of fruits and vegetables and supplement with a good fiber such as ground flax seed.

Set up the best possible support system you can (family, friends, a nursing service on standby if you can afford it). No one should have to recover from surgery without the support of other people. I was fortunate enough to have family and friends, including a wife. But being very anxious about surgery, I also signed up with a home nursing service. Basically they came and met me, signed me up (for free), and told me I could call them out at any time, day or night, for

How I Changed My Gender ...

$45 per visit. It gave me tremendous peace of mind to know they were out there. It's often impossible to reach a doctor or surgeon on the phone, so having a nurse to talk to can feel like a lifesaver.

I ended up calling the nursing service in on two occasions. Both times they just reassured me, checked my dressings and vitals, and assured me that in fact I was *not* dying and did not have to go to emergency or page my surgeon. So basically I paid them to deal with my anxiety issues, and it was well worth it. I was also fortunate that my extended benefits covered this service, provided that my doctor gave me a note saying I needed it. Especially if you will be largely on your own during recovery, finding a service like this could be really helpful and reassuring.

Another big support was being in touch with online transgender surgery support groups (see the final chapter, which is about online resources). On a few occasions I was able to send out messages about my post-surgery anxieties, and was helped a lot by the informative and supportive messages I got back.

Chapter 7: Top Surgery

For many transmen, the only surgery they ever have will be top surgery: removing the breasts, creating a male-contoured chest, and resizing the nipples to be smaller. This is mainly because having breasts clearly defines someone as female, and makes it very hard to pass as male. Many men bind their breasts, but this can be painful and even cause broken ribs in some extreme cases. Also, it usually does not allow you to get away with activities such as swimming.

Personally, I was precluded from swimming for several years, until I had my top surgery. I had very large breasts, so once testosterone caused my face to look completely male, I could not go swimming without being perceived as a freak. I found that very tough, as I love swimming. My top surgery was the hardest thing I have ever done, but it was well worth it as it changed my silhouette and my life, and freed me up to enjoy swimming again.

The kind of chest reconstruction you have will depend on the size and skin condition of your breasts. Personally I have been through both breast reduction and bilateral mastectomy. Both were extremely unpleasant experiences, and both were utterly worthwhile – I would do them both again if I had to. Even though my nipples have now been completely removed from my body and reattached twice! They have not come through these experiences unscathed: I pretty much have no sensation in them. But fortunately, that is fine with me. They were not very sensate even before they were so roughly treated.

Breast Reduction

Some men can get away with just breast reduction, if they have very tiny breasts. This is unusual though. It is also common for men to have breast reduction because that is all they can access, and then years later have a mastectomy. I went this route, as it happens. It meant I had two traumatic surgeries instead of one. I would recommend against this is you can avoid it, but generally, no one actually plans to do it this way.

I heard many anecdotes that reduction was worse than mastectomy, but that was not my experience. My reduction was a horrible experience that took six weeks to recover from, and my mastectomy was a three times as horrible experience that took three times as long to recover from. The reduction felt like I had been run over by a car, and the mastectomy felt like I had been run over by a truck that then backed up over me again. But then, I am really not good at dealing with surgeries, and I was twenty years older when I had my mastectomy done. Some men sail through all this as easily as I get through having a root canal.

BILATERAL MASTECTOMY (DOUBLE INCISION METHOD)

Bilateral mastectomy is for men with large breasts (large B and bigger) and poor skin elasticity. Bilateral mastectomies yield very satisfactory results, usually. They allow for complete removal of breast tissue, creating a very masculine shape. They also allow for repositioning of the nipples, as well as reducing the size of the nipples. All in all, a very pleasing, masculine appearance is usually achieved.

The downside to bilateral mastectomies is that it is major surgery (although it is technically termed minor surgery as it deals only with "superficial" tissues), nipple sensation is usually lost, and scarring is extensive. It basically looks like someone has cut you open from armpit to armpit – and this is because someone *has* cut you open from armpit to armpit.

I had this kind of surgery, and I am happy with the result. I don't have a perfect chest, but it is good enough. Certainly when I am dressed, my chest appears one hundred percent male. I don't flaunt it without a shirt however, because it's not perfect, and I have visible scars. Nonetheless, a bilateral mastectomy is one of the best things that ever happened to me. It opened the door to feeling comfortable in my body and passing as a man in all circumstances. And I can see and feel my pecs now!

KEYHOLE SURGERY

This is for those fortunate men who have really small breasts (middle B and smaller) and good skin elasticity (i.e. they are young and/or have not been binding for years). However it may not be as effective in terms of end results. It is less invasive, but may yield less impressive results.

During this procedure, a small incision is made along the bottom of the areola, and the breast tissue is removed with liposuction through this incision. With keyhole surgery, the nipple stalk is usually left intact, though some surgeons will resize the nipple itself. The areola is not resized. Nerve sensation is maintained.

Keyhole top surgery is typically an outpatient surgery that lasts two to three hours. General anesthesia is used.

Limitations of this method include:

- Nipple position cannot be controlled with the Keyhole procedure. It is not uncommon for the nipple areolar complex to actually become lower on the chest once the breast tissue is removed.
- The nipple areolar complex cannot be safely resized without potentially causing blood supply to the nipple to become compromised, leading to the "death" of the nipple. Therefore, the nipple size is usually not changed.

RECOVERING FROM TOP SURGERY

Your surgeon will tell you that healing times vary, but that many transmen return to desk jobs after two weeks. I have heard of people who have done this, but I think they must be supermen! It took me about six weeks before I felt ready to return to work. However, everyone is different, and I was in my fifties, which did not help.

I also had some internal bleeding on the right side of my chest after my surgery. I was kept in the recovery room for extra time, until the surgeon was sure that he did not have to cut me open again and repair anything. In the meantime, blood oozed internally, giving me a massive bruise that lasted for weeks. Fortunately, he did not have to open me up again, as the bleeding finally stopped.

When I finally got up from the bed, I had lost so much blood that I immediately fainted. It took me another two hours to get up and get to the car. In the meantime, our car had been towed, because of course with all this drama my wife forgot she was parked in the medical pickup zone. But she sorted it all out and got me home safely, while I was so woozy that I had little idea what was going on.

My point here is to make sure you have someone reliable to get you home after your surgery. The hospital will not even allow you to leave on your own, and for good reason – you will not be in any state to drive, and you may not even be in any shape to take a cab on your own. I definitely wasn't. You cannot foresee what may go wrong, so make sure you are prepared.

Some online support groups give you the opportunity to reach out and ask for help if you don't have a support person (see the final chapter on Online Resources). I once volunteered to pick up a man who had no support at all, and get him to his hotel room. I did that, and it was not easy, as he was a lot bigger than me, and very out of it. I picked him up, got his prescription meds for him, and got him into his room and into bed. In retrospect I actually feel really bad about it. That was before my own top surgery, and I did not realize what an ordeal it was. If I had known, I would not have left him alone that day.

Don't believe anyone who tells you that this is minor surgery and not a big deal. It really is a big deal to have large amounts of tissue removed from your body under general anesthesia. And sometimes, things don't go so well. So take good care of yourself, and make sure there is someone else to take care of you if you need it.

Your surgeon should give you guidelines about recovering from top surgery. Follow them religiously. In general, you should not do any heavy lifting, and should avoid lifting your arms over your head and weight training for at least four to six weeks. Light physical activity, such as walking, is a good idea.

After a bilateral mastectomy, you may have one or two medical drains. These are small tubes that line the length of the incisions, under the skin, and exit through a small incision under each arm, with a reservoir bulb attached at the ends to collect excess blood and lymphatic fluid. These drains are left in for several days to a week or more, and need to be emptied a few times a day. It's possible to do it yourself, but much better to have someone help you. You will need to return to the surgeon's office to have them removed. It will be a very happy day when that happens. I had one of mine for a week, and the other one for almost three weeks (on the side where I had bruising). They are extremely awkward and unpleasant. On the other hand, it was good to see all the excess blood from my bruised right side drain out. I was also very lucky because my very un-nurse-like wife was a wonderful support with them, doing all the upkeep and emptying them out for me several times a day.

Many surgeons require patients to wear a compression binder after surgery, for anywhere from one to six weeks. The binder helps prevent fluid build-up, assists the skin in adhering back to the chest wall, and also helps to minimize scars. I wore mine for the full six weeks, and was extremely happy to see the back of it. It's not at all fun to wear, but I think it did help my recovery.

I got myself a reclining chair before I had my top surgery, and was very glad I did it. I ended up sleeping in it for four weeks. If you sleep in a bed, you have to use a lot of upper body movement to get out of it. With a recliner, you can minimize this. This avoids any risk to your sutures and your healing process. That chair became a kind of security blanket and safe spot for me. It took quite an effort of will to return to my bed, even though my wife was in it.

Scar Care

There are numerous products you can buy for scar care. In my experience, none of them actually work. But that's just my opinion, after having spent hundreds of dollars and still having scars. Others may be more fortunate. Again, my age probably did not help. There are people whose scars disappear completely.

It is essential to follow any scar-care instructions your surgeon gives you, and to keep the scars well moisturized.

CHAPTER 8: BOTTOM SURGERY

OPTIONS FOR CREATING A PENIS

Not all transmen have bottom surgery; in fact, the majority do not, for a variety of reasons. Both routes are hard: bottom surgery is tough on the body, and not having surgery requires a high degree of personal confidence in one's own masculinity.

Surgery is subject to many complications, and often costs almost as much as buying a house (and certainly a lot more than buying a car). Also, most medical insurers do not cover it. The end result is often a very happy transman who is more than satisfied with the looks and functionality of his new penis; however, satisfactory outcomes are by no means guaranteed. I have never met a transman who said he regretted the surgery.

If you choose to do without bottom surgery, of course this is also a tough route. It's where I am right now, and I am pretty sure that will not change. Essentially it means choosing to live as a man without a penis in a world that pretty much equates a man with a penis. Our language is full of evidence of this. In literature the penis is often referred to as "his manhood" – as if that small organ embodies the sum total of all that makes him a man. And of course, testicles are almost universally equated with male courage, as in "He hasn't got the balls to …" or "Time to man up and grow a pair." I decided to research this one day: within the space of just one day, I counted 37 times that manhood was equated to either a penis or testicles (TV shows, a book I was reading called *Game of Thrones*, and conversations). This can be very depressing for a man who has neither a penis nor testicles, if you let it get to you. Not to mention that lacking those parts makes for some incredibly tense moments in locker rooms. Essentially, it is not safe for me to ever get naked in all-male environments, which I find tough, as a swimmer and an athlete.

One person who I came out to as trans many years ago asked if I was going to get a penis. When I said probably

How I Changed My Gender …

not, she replied with: "What's the point then?" For her, as for many other people, a man without a penis is not a man. Since then, I have learned not to answer personal questions like that. It's nobody's business but mine. I usually pack, so no one actually knows what's in my pants, and that's the way I like it.

But I have spent a lot of time thinking about that woman's response, and this is what I came up with (what I *should* have replied, if my mind was lighting fast!) I should have asked her if she would cease to be a woman if, God forbid, she should get breast cancer and have her breasts removed. Of course, she would not cease to be a woman, she would simply become a woman without breasts (those quintessential makers of femininity). I even knew a terribly unfortunate woman who had all of her feminine parts removed due to cancer: breasts, womb, uterus, ovaries, and vagina. The poor woman died from the cancer within a few months. However, she remained a woman, a mother, a daughter, and a sister until the day she died, regardless of the lack of those biological markers. No one questioned her gender identity, because on another level, we all know perfectly well that gender happens in our brains, not our bodies.

This is what I hang onto at this time, and most of the time I do pretty well with it. However, if they ever figure out a way to simply give me a shot that will cause my clitoris to grow into the penis it was supposed to be, I will be first in line! I have also been interested to see that in March 2015 it was reported that surgeons in South Africa are perfecting penis transplants. A case was reported on, in which a young man had full use of his new penis within four months of surgery. This kind of surgery is often necessary in South Africa, because many of the young men go through non-medical circumcision in their teen years, as part of a coming of age ritual. Every year, hundreds of them lose their penises due to post-circumcision infection. Obviously this is quite devastating for them, and some even commit suicide. Also, some of them die from the post-surgical infections.

Of course, it will be a long time, if ever, before this

kind of transplant is available to transmen. And there is the issue of finding donors, as well. But I am keeping an eye on developments in this field, as a transplant would seem to offer the most promising outcome.

In the meantime, there are a range of other surgical alternatives available for transmen. If you have the health, money, and courage to pursue this kind of surgery, there are basically two types of penis construction:

1. metoidioplasty (commonly called meta); and
2. phalloplasty (commonly called phallo).

There are many variations on these, but those are the basic choices.

There is tremendous debate and disagreement about which of these is the better choice, but fundamentally it comes down to your own personal choices and your financial resources. It is a major decision though, so take your time with it, and research as much as possible.

Phallo involves taking skin from elsewhere and creating an adult-sized penis, usually with assisted-erection capability. On the other hand, meta works with existing genitals, releases the clitoris and does some re-arranging, effectively creating a very small penis that is almost guaranteed to be orgasmic and to be able to become erect (it becomes erect before the surgery, too, but without the release this is harder to see).

The difference in a nutshell is that phallo requires much more surgery and therefore costs far more and has far more potential for complications, but usually results in being able to pass more completely as a bio man – but with a risk of losing tactile sensation and sexual sensation. On the other hand, meta requires far less surgery, is much cheaper and has far less complications – but will not result in a penis that looks adult-sized (except for some exceptionally lucky transmen who start off with enormous clitorises).

Note that the biggest meta may be four inches, while the smallest phallo may also be four inches, so the procedures are less different than is sometimes thought. Also, many men with phallo swear that they have excellent sexual sensation, and are offended at the assumption that men with phallo have less sensation than men with meta. This of course also comes down to the skill of the surgeon and the techniques used to preserve sexual sensation.

Both kinds of bottom surgery may be combined with creating stand-to-pee capacity by lengthening the urethra. Both can also be combined with the creation of testicles (scrotoplasty). This is seen by many as important for a variety of reasons, not least the fact that testicles are very effective in creating a natural looking package, so that one does not have to pack.

Following is an overview of these two surgical procedures.

METOIDIOPLASTY

Often referred to as "meta" because metoidioplasty is so hard to say. This term means "a surgical change toward the male." Metoidioplasty is a surgical procedure based on the fact that testosterone treatment usually causes the clitoris to grow longer, often to about the length of one's thumb. In this surgery, the surgeon cuts the ligament that holds the clitoris in place, and cuts away some of the surrounding tissue. In this way, a small phallus is created from the clitoris. Metoidioplasty is sometimes referred to as a "clitoris release." The clitoris is freed from some of the surrounding tissue and brought forward, to make it look like a small penis. Fat may be removed from the pubic mound and the skin may be pulled upward to bring the phallus even more forward.

Metoidioplasty may also include a urethral lengthening procedure to allow the patient to urinate through the penis while standing. This may involve using tissue from the vaginal area or from inside the mouth to create the urethral extension. Usually, a catheter has to be placed inside the urethral extension for two to three weeks while the body heals and adapts.

Typical operating time for a metoidioplasty procedure is from three to five hours, and there may be follow-up procedures and revisions later. Recovery time is usually between two to four weeks of very limited activity.

The main advantage of this procedure is that the resulting penis is natural looking and can become erect on its own, as the clitoris is made of erectile tissue, exactly like a penis. In biological terms, a penis is really just a very overgrown clitoris. Also, there are no visible scars on other parts of the body.

The disadvantages are that the resulting penis is usually quite small, and as such usually cannot be used for penetration. It also may not be a good choice for a transman whose clitoris has not grown substantially as a result of testosterone therapy (most surgeons recommend being on testosterone therapy for at least six months to two years in order to maximize growth of the clitoris). And, as with any surgery, there are potential risks of complication, such as the extrusion of testicular implants, the formation of a stricture (an abnormal narrowing or blockage) or fistula (an abnormal connection or leakage) in the newly constructed urethral passage, and potential problems of infection and tissue death (though tissue death is less common in metoidioplasty as compared to phalloplasty).

It's important when considering a metoidioplasty procedure, that you think about whether you might later want to have phalloplasty (if it turns out the neo phallus is too small for you liking). If you think this is a possibility, discuss it with your surgeon before the surgery. Various forms of surgery will leave you with different options later.

PHALLOPLASTY

Phalloplasty is the construction of a penis. Skin from other parts of your body is used to do this. Donor sites include the abdomen, groin, leg, forearm, or side of the upper torso. Phalloplasty is usually accompanied by a urethral lengthening procedure so that you can urinate through the new penis. Erections are achieved with a rod implanted permanently or inserted temporarily, or with an implanted pump device.

Phalloplasty techniques vary widely, and are improving

all the time, as microsurgery advances. You should research very carefully to decide which surgeon and technique you wish to choose. Of the various techniques, it is often said that the forearm free flap phalloplasty and the MLD flap phalloplasty result in the most realistic-looking penis of the options currently available.

PROS AND CONS OF PHALLOPLASTY

It's a very big deal to have a phalloplasty. There will be enormous costs and multiple surgical procedures, visits, and revisions. There may be major scarring, there will definitely be major recovery time, there will be pain and plenty of discomfort, and there are many risks, including tissue death and loss of all or part of the new phallus. Erotic sensation may be compromised or changed. Most neo phalluses do not have erotic sensation (although the clitoris is usually retained, beneath the new penis).

More often than not, phalloplasty is not covered by insurance.

On the plus side, phalloplasty is the only way for most transmen to achieve a penis that will pass in a locker room, that he can urinate through, and use for penetrative sex. Also, psychologically, many transmen do not feel complete without a penis.

This can be a tough decision for many transmen. Most transmen would choose to have a penis that looks and behaves as much like a biological man's penis as possible. But the costs (financial, physical, and emotional) are great, so it must be evaluated very carefully. Personally I have not gone this route, because I am older, I don't do surgery well, and I am afraid the outcome would not be good. Also, my wife is not crazy about the idea, for various reasons. And I can live without it. But I do respect that many men cannot.

If you are battling with this decision, consider joining online support and information groups to explore your options and discuss them with other transmen. Some sites offer multiple photographs contributed by other transmen, so that you can get an idea of potential outcomes. You might also consider attending the Gender Odyssey Conference, which takes place annually in the summer in Seattle. There you can speak to other men who have had this procedure, and also possibly meet some of the surgeons. Some men may even be prepared to show you their results, so that you can make an informed decision.

SCROTOPLASTY

Scrotoplasty is the creation of a scrotum. This is sometimes done by inserting testicular implants inside the labia majora, then joining the labia to create a scrotal sac.

It may also be achieved by using tissue from the thigh or abdomen to cerate a scrotal sac. Fat may be harvested from the pubic mound and transplanted into the sac, rather than using silicone implants. However, often this does not produce adequate size and symmetry.

CHAPTER 9:
GYNECOLOGICAL SURGERIES

HYSTERECTOMY

Many transmen have hysterectomies. Some because they want the female parts out for psychological reasons, and many because it means one's body won't produce any more estrogen, so testosterone doses can possibly be reduced. Before and after a hysterectomy your testosterone levels should be monitored by your endocrinologist, to see how the surgery impacts your levels, and whether you can cut down your testosterone. The up side of lower doses is there is less stress on your liver and kidneys, which are the organs that deal with drugs of any kind.

To my mind, a hysterectomy also eliminates a war between testosterone and estrogen in the body. Also, no one knows the long-term effects of high doses of testosterone on female reproductive organs, but there is a lot of speculation that it could cause elevated cancer risk. Also, some men have hysterectomies because the jurisdiction in which they live requires them to have this before they can have their legal identity changed to male.

Finally, having a complete hysterectomy means you no longer have to go for female-type tests such as pap smears. These kinds of tests are hard for most transmen, and can be hugely traumatic for some. So much so that some avoid them, and this definitely raises the risk of cancer. There is even the horror story of Robert Eads, a transman who died in 1999 because he could not find a doctor to treat him for his ovarian cancer early enough. He finally got medical care in 1997, but it was too late to save his life. Over twenty different doctors refused to treat him because they did not want him in their waiting rooms, or they did not want to have to deal with him (Kailey). The film *Southern Comfort* (2001) deals with Eads's last year, and is well worth watching. Sadly, Eads had been advised years before that he did not need a hysterectomy as he was transitioning late in life. In fact, it was this story that finally caused me to make up my mind to have a complete hysterectomy at the age of 52 (a year younger than Eads was when he died).

One down side of hysterectomy is that it is of course irreversible, meaning that the option of ever having biological children is gone (unless one can afford to freeze one's eggs).

Another down side is that it's surgery. And in my experience, surgery is always worse than the surgeon tells you it will be. Sometimes a lot worse. Every surgery carries a risk of death, infection, and complications. Every surgery requires down time when you lose muscle mass and can become depressed due to lack of exercise, or lose money due to not working. Every surgery costs money, unless you are lucky enough to have it covered. And some transmen get into a legal Catch 22 because their gender identity has been changed to male, and their insurance won't fund hysterectomies for males! Others are stuck because there is no "medical reason" for the hysterectomy.

I was lucky enough to be seen by a surgeon who specialized in transmen, and who got around the system by cleverly using privacy privilege. He would state that in his opinion it was medically required (and he was telling the truth), but he would not give details, as this would violate patient confidentiality. The insurers had no choice but to pay. However, most doctors won't do this, and many insurers won't buy it. Generally, as with all trans surgeries, you need to network and research and find out what your options are to get this surgery funded. It is different in different places, and changes over time as well.

ABDOMINAL HYSTERECTOMY

The old fashioned kind of hysterectomy (which is still commonly performed) requires slicing through abdominal walls of muscle, and therefore is very painful and hard to recover from. However, it has the advantage that almost any decent surgeon can do a very good job of it, because you are cut open and he can easily remove the organs.

By contrast, laparoscopic hysterectomy is very highly skilled work. I had a laparoscopic hysterectomy, and I was the first one of the surgeon's slate for the day, because as his receptionist told me, these are the most challenging surgeries and he liked to do them when he was fresh in the morning. It basically entailed three small cuts in my abdomen, and a (presumably) large cut at the top of the vaginal cavity. I have my cover story ready in case anyone ever notices the abdominal scars – old sword fight injury! But seriously, the scars are identical to a laparoscopic appendectomy, so that would probably be a better cover story.

The full name of my surgery was a total laparoscopic hysterectomy and bilateral salpingo-oophorectomy – which basically meant they took out everything, including womb, uterus, ovaries, tubes, and cervix. To get the uterus out, the surgeon had to insert tools into me and cut up the uterus, then pull it out piece by piece. They call this morcelating. You can see why it is more challenging than taking the organs out whole through a giant incision. Also, they have to fill your abdomen with gas so that they can better see what is going on. This means that you spend the next few days trying to get the gas out.

There are only two ways for the gas to exit (mouth and anus), and neither of those is pleasant. I had excruciating cramps in my lower belly for days, until one day I was on the toilet and passed gas with such enormous force that I actually levitated off the seat. Certainly one of the less dignified moments of my life, but well worth it for the relief that ensued. Interestingly (to me), the gas I passed smelled like a helium balloon. Fortunately for me, no one was around to see my rocket-powered ascent, or the (unfortunately) girlish scream that escaped me when it happened. The expression "tear you a new one" had never seemed quite so real before!

My surgeon implied that recovery from the surgery would be a breeze, because of the lack of giant incisions across my abdomen. Well, the reality is that my inside was full of incisions and stitches, and recovery was anything but a breeze. I had no bleeding for two weeks, then sudden fresh, red blood that terrified me (and of course it happened on a Sunday, when I could not phone the surgeon's office). I also did not have too much pain from about day three to day thirteen, and then I had a lot of brand new, fresh pain. It turned out all of this was normal, and that the key is to rest, even when you start to feel better. I had exerted myself a little on day thirteen, and I paid for it with days of pain and bleeding. So take the six weeks recovery advice *seriously*, and rest a lot, and don't do anything strenuous at all, up to and including not lifting anything heavier than a tea cup, and not driving stick (the last-mentioned was what caused my renewed pain and bleeding).

The up side was that as I gradually started to recover from my hysterectomy, it did slowly dawn on me that my body was now less female and more male than ever before. I even decided to celebrate by growing out my mustache and beard! (That only lasted a while – I got over it after a while. Unfortunately, I don't have a great abundance of facial hair.)

SPECIFIC TIPS FOR RECOVERING FROM A HYSTERECTOMY

- Have a supply of sanitary pads (sadly, these will be necessary if you don't want to bleed all over your bed.) Be prepared for the depression that may come from having to wear pads again!

- Expect to bleed a lot. They did not warn me about this, but it turns out you can bleed at any time for weeks after the surgery. You may lose quite a lot of blood, so try to eat foods that will replace lost red blood cells (such as red meat). The blood seems to stop and start, which I found alarming, but which is apparently normal. At 2.5 weeks out I experienced a small volcano of blood and clots, which scared me greatly, but apparently fits under the vast umbrella of "normal." Expect the pain to come and go as well – I thought it was all clear at day 3, and it came back at day 13. Then it lingered for weeks, although it was never severe. Don't worry about the blood unless you are filling a pad within one hour, or the discharge is smelly, or you have a fever, or you are throwing up a lot. If any of these things happen, you likely need to call 911 or go to emergency.

- When you're laying in supplies, get a lot of soap: hygiene is extremely important while recovering from this surgery. Keep your hands and body as clean as you possibly can, and shower every day (but stay out of the tub until your doctor gives the all-clear on that.) The last thing you want is any kind of bacteria entering your body

- Make sure you have loose fitting pants and undershorts. You will most likely not want to have anything tight over the lower abdomen, which is where most of the surgical activities have occurred.

- Rest up, even when you are feeling better. It is very easy to overdo things, especially with Laparoscopic surgery, because the traumatic changes to your body are less visible. The minute you overdo it, you will set yourself back, so it's not worth it.

- Try to follow the advice of not lifting anything heavier than a teacup for six weeks. You can tear your internal stitches if you lift something too heavy. That can be minor, but it can also be very serious, even life threatening.

- If you are feeling nervous, call someone, or check online. I found the many online discussions quite reassuring, and they helped me to stay calm, rather than panic. Of course you will often be in forums where everyone is calling each other "sister" and "ladies," but just man up and ignore that!

- If you had a laparoscopic hysterectomy, expect to have cramps. I was told to expect them to manifest as pain in my upper body, but I never had any of that. What I did have was painful gas in the usual place (colon), which made it impossible for me to even sit for about a week. The gas took three weeks to go away completely, and in the meantime often gave me random, painful cramps.

- If you had an adnominal hysterectomy, expect to have difficulty getting in and out of bed. Some people find that cushions, a foam wedge or sleeping in a recliner helps.
- I have heard of people who felt their internal organs "sloshing around." I did not feel that. However, it is absolutely true that organs have been removed and that your internal organs are busy re-arranging themselves. This is part of the reason why it is so vital to rest and take it easy. You do not want things flopping around and ending up where they should not be. Remember that cavity is full of things that cannot interact with each other in a comfortable way, such as colon and bladder and abdomen. You do not want things that should be in one of those places getting into the other place. Which brings me to the most important point of all.
- Whatever you do, do not have any sex that involves inserting anything of any kind into your vagina! This can result in tearing of the stitches at the top of the vagina, infection, and even death. I read about a person (a woman) who had sex with her husband and ended up with semen in her abdomen, accompanied by horrific, life-threatening infection and dehydration.

Note: this surgery can be especially traumatic for transmen as it is a "female surgery". There are many horror stories or men with beards being called "she" in hospital, or of transmen being put on a ward with a lot of women, all discussing their hysterectomies. I was immensely fortunate to be in a hospital that regularly dealt with transmen, and every single person was respectful and used the correct pronouns. *I had a nurse who called me "he" while she was inserting a catheter into my vagina!* You don't get much more trans sensitive than that – I mean, there was evidence of my biological femaleness staring her in the face, and still she stuck to "he." That reminds me, I must send her chocolates!

Oophorectomy

This is removal of the ovaries, and is often called a bilateral salpingo-oophorectomy – which just means they take the ovaries from both sides. It is usually performed at the same time as the hysterectomy.

Vaginectomy

As its name implies, this is removal of the vagina, usually performed in conjunction with various methods of creating a penis and testicles. It is not commonly performed with a hysterectomy – on the contrary, the vagina then comes in extremely handy, as it may be used to take out the internal organs.

Chapter 10: Washroom Woes

Gender theorist Judith/Jack Halberstam has identified washrooms as one of the key problems of our gendered society. Just two washrooms are not enough for the spectrum of genders we have in society. Anyone who has gone through transitioning will be intensely aware of this problem. In mid transition one's gender identity can be very ambiguous, and there are simply no washrooms marked "Ambiguous." It's "Men" or "Women" and nothing in-between!

And there is another reason why washroom needs can be one of the most intensely difficult things for many transmen: because most of us can't pee standing up. This causes emotional problems for some, and practical problems for many. Some men solve the problem by getting genital surgery. Some don't. For those of us who have not had genital surgery, this chapter is full of ideas about how to deal with this situation.

My transition journey so far has been like a hilly country – full of ups and downs, joys and woes. One of the big downers for the first few years was definitely the washroom issue. Everyone needs to use the washroom – some, like me, more often than others. So what do you do if you're out in public and there isn't a washroom that's safe and comfortable for you? That's the situation many transmen are in during their early years of transition.

For some it's just a few weeks – people who transition very fast. For those like me who transition more slowly, the discomfort can persist for months or years. For the longest time I kept using the women's washroom, because I just lacked the confidence to go to the men's. But finally, after about four years on testosterone, there came a time when every trip to a women's washroom was traumatic. I would try to scoot in when no one was around. When I was ready to exit, I would skulk in the stall until the washroom sounded empty, and then rush out without even stopping to wash my hands.

Causing Little Old Ladies to
Faint in the Washroom ...

Then things got worse. I started having experiences where women were visibly upset to bump into me in the washroom. On one memorable occasion, a little old lady almost fainted. On another, in a pub, a woman very nearly got into a fist fight with me as she jealously guarded the door to "her" washroom.

I finally realized that I had reached the stage where it was no longer possible to use the women's washroom. That seems to be how it is with transition – it happens kind of slowly, and then one day you look in the mirror and realize that you just cannot pass for the gender you are leaving behind any more. That's a very joyful moment for most of us – certainly it was for me – but it did bring with it the scary realization that women's washrooms were no longer an option. At that point I had no choice but to brave the men's room.

Using the Men's Room – A Beginner's Guide

Once I started using the men's room, I wished I'd started a lot sooner. Sure, the first time was scary. And the second and the third. But it soon dawned on me that no one was taking the slightest bit of notice of me. This had the enormous advantage that no one was going to faint, or pick a fight with me at the door. In fact, it turned out that the men's room was a lot more comfortable than the women's room, where people had been staring at me for a long time. In general, men look at each other less in washrooms than women. There's a whole different dynamic going on. Most men in washrooms are indifferent, or they simply want to make it clear they aren't gay. On the other hand, most women are (rightfully) suspicious of some men, so they really tend to notice if there's a man in their washroom. The bottom line is that you will be less likely to be noticed in the men's room than in the women's room.

Of course, it wasn't perfect. For starters, men's rooms

are often dirtier and smellier than woman's rooms. Especially if you have to sit. A pub on a busy night can be absolutely brutal – you may find yourself wishing you could scrub down the seat. But it's not an option, so you just have to man up and deal with it. Remember, other people's urine cannot kill you.

Once you are in the washroom, if you cannot urinate standing up, you do of course have to use a stall. Which sometimes means waiting for a while. If so, find an inconspicuous place to stand, and then attempt to look as if you are looking at nothing and no one, and are in fact unaware that there are any people at all around you. Whatever you do, do *not* watch other men using the urinal!

Once in the stall, you know what to do – sit down and pee! However, I was initially rendered pee-shy by the fear of being heard to pee while sitting down (because the guy in the next stall can usually see that your feet are facing the wrong way). But over the years I have learned a thing or two, which I thought I would pass on.

TIPS FOR TRANSMEN USING MEN'S ROOMS

First of all, bear in mind that you will be nowhere near as conspicuous as you will feel. Assuming that you pretty much pass, it is likely that no one is going to take the slightest bit of notice of you.

Second, take comfort in the knowledge that there actually are bio men who sit down to pee. Yes, really. So, in the unlikely event that anyone takes enough notice of you to realize you're doing this, they're just going to assume you are one of those men. However, in years of using the men's room I have never once had any indication that anyone noticed. I have never had a strange man question me about my bathroom activities. After all, if someone did say something, I would have every right to ask: "Why were you watching me in the washroom?" … a question that very few men want to hear.

Third, in the beginning it's a good idea at the beginning to use men's washrooms that fit one of two extremes: either very quiet, or very busy. The first kind is a no-brainer – if

How I Changed My Gender ...

there's no one else there, there's nothing to worry about. Especially the single-use ones, such as those that are available at Starbucks.

The very busy kind was a surprise to me. You'd think a room packed with other men would be more intimidating, but it turns out that the busy kind – such as the ones at the big movie houses – are the easiest of all. This is because they're so noisy. You can sit in your stall and urinate noisily away, secure in the knowledge that the guy in the next stall does not know you are peeing because he cannot hear you! These are my favorite kind of washroom. The middle-sized ones are the scariest, as you will probably have company, and they will likely be able to hear you. Still, if you follow the basic rules, you should be fine.

Something to watch out for are sting operations. I am pretty sure I was targeted by one in Sears, of all places. It was in the early days of my transition, and I was kind of lurking around near the men's room, simply because I wanted to be sure it was empty before I went in. I guess store security saw me and misinterpreted my reasons for lurking. I had no sooner unzipped and was trying to use my STP device, than a guy rushed in, starting unzipping beside me, and said, "How you doing?" while looking right at me. I had already had enough experience of men's rooms to know that men never do that. Therefore either he was trying to pick me up (I like to think that, but he probably wasn't), or he was part of a sting operation to see if I was trying to pick up someone in the washroom. My response was shock and horror, I mumbled something incoherent, zipped up and left. Not sure whether he took that for innocence or guilt, but obviously there was no cause to arrest me!

Which brings me to a key point: it's essential that you know the rules of men's washrooms before you venture in. These are pretty simple.

Basic Rules for Transmen Using the Men's Room

- Walk in like you own the place.
- Do not talk to anyone.
- Do not make eye contact with anyone.
- Do not look at any one. If you have to for some reason, keep it brief, as if you are acknowledging the existence of an equal who you don't really care about, and will forget the instant he is out of your sight.
- Do your stuff and get out of there.
- While seated on the toilet, keep your feet widely spaced (so as to create the impression of making space for your testicles).
- Never, never look at another guy's genitals. (This is the most important rule of all!)
- If you are able stand to pee thanks to surgery or using an STP, try not to choose a urinal that is directly next to another man who is peeing.
- If you are in a small washroom and you are forced to stand right next to someone else, keep your eyes forward and don't touch his elbow or any other part of his body.
- Never make eye contact with someone else while at standing at a urinal. If it is a co-worker he may well talk to you casually, but he probably won't look you in the eyes, and you should do the same.

Warning About Using the Men's Room

Never assume you cannot be seen, just because you are in a stall. For one thing, porcelain tiles often reflect, so your reflection might be visible to the guy in the next stall. For another thing, doors in men's washrooms are often less than well fitted, and your privacy is likely to be compromised. Also, a lot of men pick up other men in washrooms, so there might be someone trying hard to see you. Given that you cannot assume privacy at any time, be very circumspect. If you haven't had bottom surgery, make sure your shirt is hanging

How I Changed My Gender ...

down to cover the fact that you don't look like the average man. If you use a packer, be careful with how you handle it – if another man sees you casually ripping your penis off, that is going to attract attention! The best thing is to be wearing special trans underwear from a place like TranZwear (see Online Resources in the final chapter). These have pouches or c-rings to hold your packer, so you can keep it tucked into your underwear while peeing. This also avoids the possibility that you will forget you are wearing a packer and drop it onto the (often filthy) floor.

I once had my packer drop out and onto the floor in the men's change room at a public swimming pool. Fortunately testosterone seems to have sharpened my reflexes, plus of course I was shocked, so I grabbed it so fast I swear my arm must have looked like a blur. In any event, no one took the slightest bit of notice (a recurring theme in men's change rooms and wash rooms). I am pretty sure no one noticed: after all, if a man were to see another man's penis apparently fall off, he would probably scream or faint, or at least look horrified. And have nightmares for years. This is after all supposed to be the primal fear of bio men!

LEARNING HOW TO STAND TO PEE

Various manufacturers make Stand to Pee (STP) devices to make it easier for us transmen to pass. I have tried most of them, and took a really long time to master them. To be frank, I have never really 100% mastered any of them. However, some men do manage it, and it's certainly worth a try.

If one device does not work for you, try another – it's not a one size fits all situation. I found it completely impossible to master the ones with a medicine spoon type fixture, but many men find they work just fine. If you want to try those, I recommend DJ knows Dicks (see Online Resources). I had my highest level of success with a device from Pee-cock Products (see Online Resources). It's a packer type device that has the balls are ingeniously formed in a hollow way so as to catch the pee and funnel it down the shaft. You press the balls firmly over yourself and pee. However, I made the mistake of first ordering the Small size. This one was just too small, and did not catch all the urine. Also, it was so short there was no way I would ever have got it clear of my pants to use a public urinal. I then over-compensated and bought the largest size, At 6.5 inches it was *really* too big. I have now given up on using these devices. However, many men find them very useful.

By the way, most of these products come with plastic rods so that they can also be used for play. I also hear that the shape of the Pee-cock products works well for men who have had meta without urethral lengthening. Pee-Cock Products also offers harnesses to wear with the Pee-Cock.

Based on my experiences with trying to learn to use STPs, and on what I have heard from other men, I offer the following advice:

- When you first use it, try it naked in the shower.
- Progress to using it naked, while standing and aiming into your home toilet.
- Then progress to using it clothed, while aiming into your home toilet. Clothed is much harder as you have to avoid wetting your pants, and you have to wiggle the device clear of your pants while not letting it lose contact with the appropriate part of your body.
- Practice! Some men find these things easy, but for most it really takes a lot of practice to get it right.
- Be sure to clean up the urine that will inevitably fall on the ground, otherwise your washroom will quickly start to smell.
- When you are ready to progress to using the STP in public, start by using it inside the stalls. A lot of men go into the stalls to stand and urinate, I suspect so that they can drop their pants further without attracting attention – the last thing you want in a men's room is to have your pants around your knees and your naked butt on show to the other men.
- Once you have mastered using it in a public stall, progress to a public urinal, if that is your aim. Bear in mind that some urinals are really high, which can

be hard for transmen who are on the shorter side. You don't want to show up at the urinal and find you can't reach it without urinating all over yourself! Check out the height before you use it.

Tip: The way some men finally master their STPs is to tell themselves that they are was not allowed to urinate unless they use their STP. If you do this, it means you have to use it every single time. Of course, this is harder to achieve if you have limited privacy at home. Using this every-time-no-excuses method, you should master it within a week, and be ready to use it in public. It's hard to change lifetime habits, but it is possible.

On the other hand, you can choose to always use the stalls. It is highly unlikely that anyone will ever notice.

CHAPTER 11:
ONLINE RESOURCES FOR TRANSMEN

GENERAL ONLINE RESOURCES

FTM Phalloplasty Info Group on Yahoo groups, at
yahoo.com/group/ftmphalloplastyinfo
This group is intended to complement the all-inclusive
FTM Surgery Info Yahoo group. This is a smaller group
dedicated to the serious discussions needed as one moves
forward with plans for a phalloplasty. All FTMs who are
seriously considering phalloplasty surgery, as well as those
who have completed a phalloplasty, are welcome. Interested
persons are required to answer a short questionnaire before
membership is granted.

FTM Surgery Info Group on Yahoo groups, at yahoo.
com/group/ftmsurgeryinfo
An extensive resource for information, photos, links,
and research materials pertaining to surgery options for
FTMs. You must apply for membership to access this
group. Includes information about the following FTM-
related procedures: metoidioplasty, phalloplasty, Centurion,
hysterectomy, vaginectomy, salpingo-oophectomy,
scrotoplasty, urethro-plasty, testicular prostheses, and
chest surgeries including double incision, liposuction,
periareolar, keyhole, non-surgical enhancement alternatives
such as pumping, stretching, piercing, and more. Interested
persons are required to answer a short questionnaire before
membership is granted.

Hudson's FTM Resource, at http://www.ftmguide.org/
In my opinion, this is one of the best resources for
transmen on the Net. Make it your home page! I learned
how to tie a tie on this website, thus impressing my wife,
who was pretty sure she was going to have to do it for
me the first time I wore a tie to a formal event. It has
information about pretty much everything, plus tons of

links. I am indebted to this site for some of the content in this book, and for a lot of help during my transition.

Man Tool, at www.lorencameron.com/mantool
An online photo-book of FTM genital surgeries. A $19.95 fee gives you viewing access for one year.

The Transitional Male, at www.thetransitionalmale.com
Check out both the Surgery Information Index and the Surgical Photo Galleries on this site.

Trans Care Project of Vancouver, British Colombia, at transhealth.vch.ca/resources/library/index.html
Completed in January of 2006, the Trans Care Project created a series of training materials and practice guidelines for clinicians treating trans patients, as well as consumer information about trans health for trans people – FTM and MTF. Their materials are downloadable in PDF, and cover numerous topics of concern to trans people and their care providers. Scroll down the page to the "Consumer Information" section to see the pamphlet "Surgery: A Guide for FTMs."

Transbucket, at www.transbucket.com
Transbucket is a repository for images of FTM gender reassignment surgery results. FTMs can upload pictures of their own surgical results, as well as search through images other transmen have submitted.

TranZwear, at http://www.tranzwear.net/
For underwear, packers, STP products, etc. This company is run by and staffed by transmen, and makes custom products to order at a very reasonable price. Basically they take items like Dockers underwear and sew on a c-ring and a cloth ball cage that hold your packer in place. You can specify all kinds of details about the products you want. The products on this website changed my life, making it possible for me to work in my new male identity without constantly worrying that people would notice I looked

"wrong." Also, the products removed my fear that I would absentmindedly drop my packer while in the washroom, or leave it behind in there. They offer outstanding products, prices, and service. I now buy all my underwear from there.

Resources for Packers

These are used to give a realistic bulge in your underwear, helping you to "pass". Some of them are cheap and simple; at the other extreme are extremely expensive and realistic prosthetics that can be glued to the skin. As a bare minimum, they should be washable. These are just a few of the available products, but include my favorite – Reel Magik.

Lola Jake, at http://www.lolajake.com/?q=node/34
Moving into the premium class, but not super expensive like some – around $200 and up. These are mainly meant to be used with medical grade adhesive. For extra money you can get one with a hole for a STP, and a rod for intercourse.

Mr. Right, at http://www.babeland.com/Mr.-Right/d/1357
Much liked by many for the realistic testicles. Around $60.

Reel Magik, at http://www.reelmagik.com/REELMAGIK/Home_Page.html
This company sells a variety of prosthetics, and has an FTM Prosthesis Store. They do extremely realistic but extremely expensive prosthetic penises. However, they also offer what they call their basic packer, which is under a hundred dollars, but pleasingly realistic as they use the same mold that they use for their medical prosthetic. It has 3-D testicles, and is in my opinion the most realistic and pleasing packer you can get for less than a hundred dollars. It straddles the line between packer and prosthetic. It also does not have to be powdered; the only maintenance it requires is an occasional wash.

STP packers are soft packers feature a length of flexible tubing through their shafts to allow the user to pee through the packer. It can be tricky to get this right. I personally do not use them, but many transmen do.

DJ Knows Dicks, at http://www.pee3.ca/
This company makes STPs that are highly recommended by many transmen. I have had excellent service from DJ. Web site includes a video showing how well these gadgets can work once you know what you're doing. DJ also makes the Pissin' Passin' Packer (PPP), at djknowsdicks.com. This item is a retrofitted soft-packer that has been modified with tubing and a medicine spoon to create a stand-to-pee packer. DJ offers 4 sizes (Teeny is 3-1/2 inches, Small is 5 inches, Medium is 6 inches, and Huge is 7 inches). All models are $50.00.)

Home Grown Packer Line, STP options, at www.hg-prosthetics.com
This is an Australian site that offers several models and sizes of soft packers, made of elastomeric gel, that can be converted into STP packers. The packers are made by an FTM community member and are sold at a very affordable price. The J Jay 4.5", Hugo 5.5", Average Joe 3.5", Johnson 6", and Peter 3.5" models can all be equipped as STP packers. The base price for J Jay, Hugo, and Johnson (without STP) is AU$100; Average Joe and Peter is AU$80. To add the STP feature, add AU$30.

Like Real Prosthetics, at www.likerealusa.com
The professionally made prosthetics offered on the Like Real site include both flaccid and erect models that are designed to be attached to the body with medical adhesive. A number of the flaccid models are equipped with an STP urination system that is built into the packer (the erect models do not have a urination system). There are flaccid models featuring the appearance of uncut foreskin, as well

as circumcised models, and they offer a choice of 5 skin tone options. The detailing is quite realistic, and you can view videos of most products to see multiple views. Like Real also offers the medical adhesive and adhesive remover needed to wear the packers affixed to the skin. Prices range from around $200 to just over $700, and they do sell sets that include both flaccid and erect prosthesis.

Pee-Cock 3-in-1 Packer, at www.peecockproducts.com
This product, introduced in 2011, is designed to be a stand-to-pee packer and pack-and-play model all in one. Made of soft silicone, the shaft of the Pee-Cock has an opening throughout its length to allow for urination. The opening through the shaft also can accommodate a flexible erection rod that is inserted through the back of the packer. The back of the packer is shaped like the opening of a funnel; it is pressed low and tightly against the body over the urethral opening during urination. Due to the shape of the funnel, the Pee-Cock may also work well for men who have had metoidioplasty. The Pee-Cock comes in three sizes, 4 inches ($129), 5.5 inches ($139), and 6.5 inches ($149). They are in the flaccid state when worn without the erection rod. There are 3 shades of skin tones available: Caucasian, moderate brown or dark brown. Pee-Cock Products also offers two harnesses to wear with the Pee-Cock.

STP-FITZ, at www.toolshedtoys.com
STP-FITZ, an FTM-owned business, retrofits soft packers into two styles of STP packer – one with a medicine spoon receptacle, and one with a softer, wider silicone nipple receptacle. All styles of STP-FITZ packers can be purchased through the Tool Shed web site, where a number of other products for transmen are also available – check the "gender expression" link on the left hand page menu for a listing. Note: Purchasing products through the Tool Shed web site directly supports FTMguide.org.

Urinall STP Packer, at www.urinall.co.uk
The Urinall is a lightweight, handmade product created

specifically for the FTM trans community. It is a small, hard funnel about the size of a large medicine spoon, but the edges are rounded and beveled for a comfortable fit. The Urinall site offers a version of the Urinall and tubing placed in a 3.5" STP packer (made from Mr. Softie by Fleshlight). Cost is £35 (that's in British pounds), which includes shipping anywhere in the world.

BIBLIOGRAPHY

Bornstein, Kate. (1995). Gender Outlaw: On Men, Women
 And The Rest Of Us. New York: Random House.
Bornstein, Kate. (1998). My Gender Workbook: How To
 Become A Real Man, A Real Woman, The Real You,
 Or Something Else Entirely. New York: Routledge.
Bornstein, Kate. Gender Outlaw: On Men, Women and the
 Rest of Us. New York: Random House, 1995.
Bornstein, Kate. My Gender Workbook: How to Become
 a Real Man, a Real Woman, The Real You, or
 Something Else Entirely. New York: Routledge, 1998.
Butler, Judith. Introduction: Rethinking Genders. Velvet
 Light Trap, 41 (1998): 2+.
Butler, Judith. (1990). Gender Trouble: Feminism and the
 Subversion of Identity. New York: Routledge.
Butler, Judith. (2003). Performative Acts And Gender
 Constitution: An Essay In Phenomenology And
 Feminist Theory. In Carole R. McCann and Seung-
 Kyung Kim. (Eds.) Feminist Theory Reader: Local
 and Global Perspectives. New York and London:
 Routledge: 415-427.
Califia, Patrick. Changes: Transgender Politics. 2nd edition.
 Cleis Press, 2003.
CBC News Online. Indepth: David Reimer. The Boy who
 Lived as a Girl. May 10, 2004. Retrieved from web
 site: http://www.cbc.ca/news/background/reimer/
Conway, Lynn. Website at http://ai.eecs.umich.edu/people/
 conway/conway.html. Conway is a famed pioneer
 of microelectronics chip design who is transgender
 (MTF). Her website is a great resource.
Cromwell, Jason. Transmen & FTMs: Identities, Bodies,
 Genders & Sexualities. Urbana and Chicago:
 University of Illinois Press, 1999.
Crow, Barbara A. and Gotell, Lise. Open Boundaries:
 A Canadian Women's Studies Reader. Toronto:
 Prentice-Hall Canada Inc., 2000.
dobkin, alix. (2002). The emperor's new gender. off our

backs, April 2000. Retrieved from web site: http://www.casac.ca/womenonly/newgender.htm.

Dworkin, Andrea. (22 Sept. 2003). Out of the Closet. New Statesman: 132+.

Edwards, Tim. (2004) Queer Fears: Against the Cultural Turn. Sexualities, 1(4), 471-484.

Fausto-Sterling, Anne. (2000). Sexing the body. New York: Basic Books.

Feinberg, Leslie. Stone Butch Blues. Los Angeles: Alyson Books, 1993.

Gauntlett, David. Theory.Org. Judith Butler. (No date). Retrieved Nov. 21, 2005 from web site: http://www.theory.org.uk/ctr-butl.htm#links.

Gorton R. Nick, et al. Medical Therapy and Health Maintenance for Transgender Men: A Guide For Health Care Providers. Available on the Internet, here.

Green, Jamison. Becoming a Visible Man.

Haas, Ann P., Rodgers, Philip L. and Herman, Jody L. Suicide Attempts among Transgender and Gender Non-Conforming Adults. Findings of the National Transgender Discrimination Survey.

Harrison, David. (1997). The Personals. In Carol Queen and Lawrence Schimel (Eds.) PoMoSexuals: Challenging Assumptions about Gender and Sexuality (pp. 129-37). San Francisco: Cleis Press.

Jagodzinski, Jan. (2003). Women's Bodies of Performative Excess: Miming, Feigning, Refusing, and Rejecting The Phallus. Journal For The Psychoanalysis Of Culture & Society, 8(1): 23+.

Jones, Aphrodite. All she Wanted: Brandon Teena: The Girl who Became a Boy but Paid the Ultimate Price. New York: Simon & Schuster, Inc., 1996.

Kailey, Matt. Just Add Hormones: An Insider's Guide to the Transsexual Experience. Boston: Beacon Press, 2005.

Kotula, Dean. The Phallus Palace: Female to Male Transsexuals. Los Angeles: Alyson Publications, 2002.

Lawrence, Anne A. Normal: Transsexual Ceos, Cross-Dressing Cops, and Hermaphrodites With Attitude. Archives of Sexual Behavior, 32. 2003.

Lorber, Judith. Gender Inequality: Feminist Theories and Perspectives. California: Roxbury Publishing Company, 2001.

Mazur, Tom. A Lovemap of a Different Sort from John Money. The Journal of Sex Research, 41.1 (2004): 115+.

Namaste, Viviane K. Invisible Lives: The Erasure of Transsexual and Transgendered People. Chicago and London: The University of Chicago Press, 2000.

Olsson, Stig-Eric and Anders R. Moller. (2003). On The Incidence and Sex Ratio of Transsexualism in Sweden, 1972-2002. Archives Of Sexual Behavior, 32.

Peters, Wendy. Queer Identities: Rupturing Identity Categories and Negotiating Meanings of Queer. Canadian Woman Studies, 24.2-3.

Salih, Sara. Judith Butler. London: Routledge, 2002.

Scott, Joan W. Deconstructing Equality-Versus-Difference: Or, the Uses of Poststructuralist Theory for Feminism. In Carole R. McCann and Seung-Kyung Kim (eds) Feminist Theory Reader: Local and Global Perspectives. New York and London: Routledge: 378-390, 2003.

Sterling, Anne-Fausto. Sexing the Body. New York: Basic Books, 2000.

Theory.org. Queer Theory. Retrieved from web site: http://www.theory.org.uk/ctr-que1.htm.

Wallen, Kim. In Memory of Robert W. Goy – Pioneering American Sex Researcher. Journal of Sex Research (May, 1999).

Wiederman, Michael W. Hermaphrodites Speak (Video). The Journal of Sex Research, 38.2 (2001): 175+.

Zhou, J., M. Hofman, L. Gooren and D. Swaab. A Sex Difference in the Human Brain and its Relation to Transsexuality. Nature 68-70 (Nov. 1995).

Made in the USA
Coppell, TX
24 February 2021

50810414R00066